From Couscous to Kasha

Reporting from the Field of
Jewish Community Work

FROM COUSCOUS TO KASHA

REPORTING FROM THE FIELD
OF JEWISH COMMUNITY WORK

SEYMOUR EPSTEIN (EPI)

URIM PUBLICATIONS
Jerusalem • New York

From Couscous to Kasha: Reporting From the Field of Jewish
Community Work
By Seymour Epstein

Printed in Israel. First Edition.
ISBN 13: 978-965-524-0177
Urim Publications
P.O. Box 52287, Jerusalem 91521 Israel

Lambda Publishers Inc.
527 Empire Blvd., Brooklyn, New York 11225 U.S.A.
Tel: 718-972-5449 Fax: 718-972-6307, mh@ejudaica.com

www.UrimPublications.com

וכי יש אדם בישראל שאין לו גואלים?
(מסכת קידושין כא)

Is there a Jew without a redeemer?
(Talmud, Tractate *Kiddushin* 21a)

CONTENTS

ACKNOWLEDGEMENTS

I WISH TO THANK MY FAMILY, my former JDC colleagues, and my current work community for their role in the writing of this book.

I could not have worked in the JDC field without the support and guidance that I received from all of my supervisors and co-workers. Ralph Goldman, Michael Schneider, Linda Levi, Steven Schwager, Asher Ostrin, Amos Avgar, Linda Pardes, Dorith Benmoha, Abby Pitkowsky, Shoshana Kligman, Evelyn Peters z"l, Stanley Abramovich, Moe Levine, Cecile Misrahi z"l, Stuart Saffer, Sarah Levin, Itzik Averbuch, Charles Hoffman z"l, Sara Bogen, Shmuel Levin, Eli Ragimov and many others created the working ethos of an organization devoted to Jewish community wherever it could flourish. Sherry Hyman and her staff in the JDC archives were wonderfully helpful.

Our two children, Yoni and Sarit, came to my wife and me in the middle of my JDC career and put up with many days of my absence at a time when they needed both parents, not just a loving mother. I hope that one day they will realize how much my thoughts were with them even though I was far away.

I wish to thank all the folks at Urim Publications for all of their assistance in getting this book into print and into the hands of the public.

The lay and professional leadership of the UJA Federation of Greater Toronto deserves great credit for granting me sabbatical leave in 2005 and 2006 so that I could work on this memoir. I could not have completed the research and writing while on a full work schedule. My colleagues at the Federation's Board of Jewish Education took over in such a fashion that the leave was a true retreat. The associate director, Yael Seliger, took on full responsibility for running the BJE in my absence, and my gratitude to her is boundless.

My highest praises and most profound gratitude go to the wondrous woman to whom I dedicate this book: Cheryl, my wife, love, and partner in all. For all the difficult and lonesome moments, for the strained phone calls from faraway places, for the constant encouragement, and for the very wisest counsel – for all of these and much more, my love and my thanks.

WHAT'S MISSING

I WISH TO SET FORTH the parameters of this book by briefly listing the events, issues, and people that do not appear in the many stories.

First: my family. While Cheryl traveled with me from time to time before we adopted Yoni and Sarit in 1991 and lived with me in Casablanca and Paris from 1986 to 1991, my family mostly stayed home during the long trips of my field experiences and coped without me. In the first years of our marriage, Cheryl was subjected to four different continents, three foreign languages, three wildly different cultures, and an absent husband!

I tried to phone home every Friday to bless my children before Shabbat, and even that was often difficult in the pre-cellphone era. Since the traditional blessing involves placing one's hands on the child's head, the only humorous aspect of my long absences was Sarit's placing the phone on her head during the long-distance blessings. While I was away "saving the Jewish people," three wonderful Jews whom I love dearly were at home in Jerusalem without me. When I left Cheryl alone in Paris, Casablanca, or Jerusalem for urgent trips to strange places, she managed heroically without me. For all of this I am very grateful. My family's absence from the book has no relation to the important part they played in my ability to get the work done.

The conflicts that JDC sometimes had within and without are also missing from this book. Any NGO with a complex mission, a central headquarters in one country, and several strong field operations elsewhere is going to experience internal conflicts and tensions. Of course, they existed in the Joint, but their ability to distract the organization from its mission or to alter the operational norms was the exception rather than the rule. Since other organizations such as the Jewish Agency for Israel, various departments of the Israeli government, Jewish community federations, and the major religious denominations overlapped with our work, conflicts inevitably arose and had to be worked out in situ. While these conflicts in themselves make for great history and some juicy stories, this book avoids most of them and deals primarily with the JDC and its dialogue with specific host communities.

Related to that is the topic of aliyah (immigration to Israel). In both Morocco and the Former Soviet Union (FSU), aliyah is the major story of the last half of the twentieth century. North African aliyah changed the face of both Israel and Moroccan Jewish life in the 1950s and 1960s. During the 1990s, one million Jews from the FSU became Israelis. While we at the JDC shared in the enthusiasm and excitement regarding these major aliyot, our mission was not directly related to aliyah. We did nothing to hinder aliyah, and in fact, some of our work in many countries helped Jews to settle in Israel. But since the grand story of those who opted for Israel and the brave souls who helped them get there is not a JDC story, it is not part of this account.

Finally, one last omission. With some exceptions, I have used neither the names of my colleagues nor those of the active members of the host communities. I would need permission to do the latter, and tracking down dozens of such people was not feasible. As to my colleagues, many of them are still working in the field and might appreciate the low-key anonymity that JDC still prefers. Again, the absence of names has nothing to do with the great respect, admiration, and gratitude I feel towards these women and men who shared my stories.

INTRODUCTION

FROM 1981 TO 1999 I was employed by the American Jewish Joint Distribution Committee (the JDC or Joint) first as a pedagogic consultant, then as a country director, and finally as director of Jewish education. The countries in which I served were Morocco, France, and the former Soviet Union (FSU). I was active in North Africa from 1981 to 1988, living there for five of those years. The JDC office in Paris, a regional headquarters, was under my supervision from 1988 to 1991, while my last years (1991–1999) were based in Jerusalem with much travel to the FSU and many other JDC operations worldwide.

I was born one year after the Holocaust in Europe and two years before the establishment of the State of Israel and spent much of my youth mourning and celebrating those two events respectively. Nevertheless, I had the sense that the great moments of twentieth-century Jewish history had passed me by and that my life would be as a passive object of that history, not one of its writers. Indeed, as a student of Hebrew literature in my early twenties I was much influenced by Haim Hazaz's short story, "The Sermon" (הדרשה) in which the anti-hero,

Yudka, bemoans the fact that Jewish history is something that is done to us. He claims we have become objects and, in his Zionist fervor, he yearns to be a subject.

My chosen career as a Jewish educator was my humble attempt to "do" Jewish history by teaching a new generation of Jewish youth about their rich heritage of languages, literature, values, and spirituality. As active as that was as a profession, it was the Joint that gave me the opportunity for proactive involvement in making new history among Diaspora Jews.

In the disintegrating atmosphere of the once-great ancient community of Morocco, in the contemporary issues of Western European communities, and in the reconnection of Soviet Jews to their Judaism I was given the privilege of being teacher, midwife, broker, caregiver, and guide to thousands of Jews and their respective communities. Like me, they had to live the second half of the twentieth century and beyond after the historic events of the first half, such as the mass migration of East European Jews to America, Palestine, and other shores, the Nazi Holocaust, and the establishment of Israel in 1948.

Those twentieth-century events resulted in the founding of the JDC in 1914 and then in the establishment of various modes of operation worldwide to help Jews in trouble. By the time I signed up as a JDC worker in 1981, the organization had grown into various kinds of operations, depending on the needs of any given community. Although most think of this American charitable organization as primarily serving the Diaspora, its Jerusalem offices were larger than its headquarters in New York and the work of Joint-Israel was enormously influential in shaping entire sections of the Israeli social landscape, with community centers (*matnasim*) and old-age facilities the best illustrations of that influence.

In ancient communities such as Morocco or India, in secret operations such as in Syria or post-1979 Iran, or in complex situations such as Communist Romania or Hungary, the Joint always managed to support the local Jews and to carry out its activities with hardly any noise or distraction. In fact, its status as one of the best-kept secrets of North American Jewish life was not helpful in raising the UJA (United Jewish Appeal) funds that it needed to support its programs.

It was this JDC that I joined in 1981 as a pedagogic consultant in Morocco. It was not clear what skills I brought to the task, since I knew very little about the organization (having assumed that it had disappeared after the post-World War II Displaced Persons camps in Europe) and even less about Morocco. I had a limited amount of high-school French and no Moroccan Arabic, though I possessed several academic degrees and spoke Hebrew. My work experience was in Jewish day-school teaching, curricular design, teacher training, and informal Jewish education; most of which had nothing in common with the schools, youth groups, and camps I would encounter in North Africa.

Surprise and dismay were the leitmotifs of my first years in the Joint.

The first question I posed to myself about the many experiences and adventures I had was how they fit together. The only factor they all share is my presence as witness (and sometimes actor). What effect did they have on me as a professional and as a Jew? Were there lessons to be learned beyond the experiences themselves? Were there morals hidden in these stories? As I answered these questions, I learned how to tell these stories and in what order to tell them.

To state things simply, the Joint did the mitzvah work of the North American Jewish community. It embodied in its mission the notion that we are ultimately responsible for one another. I remember well an evening in Irkutsk, Siberia after a day of taking some JDC board members to visit homebound, elderly Jews who were being assisted by a local Jewish welfare organization funded by the Joint. The evening news on television included a report from a journalist who had accompanied us that day. She told the local audience that American Jews had come to see their charity investment, and then added her own editorial, saying, "If only we Russians might learn a lesson from this kind of brotherly love and concern that spans oceans!" Not only did we act on our responsibility. Not only did we teach this lesson to a new Jewish community that had just emerged from the kind of persecution that had distanced Jews from their innate values – but we also managed to ascend into another realm of mitzvah, *ohr la-goyim*, becoming a light to other nations.

The operational values with which we entered communities as JDC workers were mainstream Jewish concepts that are worth listing and illustrating.

תלמוד תורה
TALMUD TORAH (JEWISH EDUCATION)

This appears first on my list not only because of my career as an educator, but also because my original posting in Casablanca was as a pedagogic consultant to the Jewish schools in Morocco. By 1991 I had become the director of Jewish education for worldwide Joint programs. In almost every country of operation, Jewish education was a JDC area of interest. Wherever we worked, the JDC recognized that Jewish education was essential to the life of a community, that it needed to pervade every aspect of communal life (right down to the Jewish calendars that went into food packages), and that Jewish learning was essential to the future of every community.

צדקה
TZEDAKA (CHARITY AND SOCIAL JUSTICE)

The Joint receives almost all of its funding from North American Jews through the United Jewish Appeal and designated donations. It is the charitable arm of North American Jewry for work in distressed Jewish communities. Our long history of concern under difficult conditions has created a communal norm of responsibility that reflects the Biblical imperative of social justice.

חסד
CHESED (COMPASSION)

While tzedaka is a matter of justice and obligation in Jewish life, chesed describes the acts of compassion and love that are beyond the letter of the law. JDC work in Jewish communities always stressed both the obligation to help and the right to do more than required. Our welfare centers in the FSU were named chasadim because we knew that Russian Jews could identify with this ancient Jewish concept even after seventy years of separation from their spiritual roots. We were told that post-Soviets would never volunteer, but within several years we had hundreds of volunteers working all over the FSU in dozens of community organizations. When JDC began its work in Morocco after World War II, its trained social workers had some lessons to learn from the local community about how chesed could complement tzedaka. As the French social workers learned that the local welfare program practiced for centuries was called hilouk ("distribution" in Hebrew), they also learned of a quiet program called nistarim (hidden), which offered discreet assistance to establishment families that had recently become impoverished.

אהבת ישראל
AHAVAT YISRAEL (LOVE OF ISRAEL)

The spirit of JDC's mission is one of love for both the people of Israel and the land of Israel. Nothing else can explain the single-minded dedication to helping Jews no matter what the consequences. There were situations when rescuing Jews meant compromising on other values and concerns (like working with a murderous dictator), but true ahavat Yisrael trumped all other considerations. On many occasions, the flow of Jewish love and its concomitant sense of responsibility coming from the JDC were met by parallel sentiments in host communities. The act of helping, in itself, was a model to other communities and personalities in the field.

תיקון עולם
TIKKUN OLAM (REPAIRING THE WORLD)

The specifics of a JDC country operation revolve around welfare, health, care for the aged, education, and cultural activity. They are linked to the value of repairing the world that is venerated in Jewish law and lore. Some of the veteran workers I encountered in my first years were embodiments of the messianic urge to fix what is broken. One of the aspects of JDC work that captivated me early on was the ability to work with million-dollar budgets for enormous projects in one moment, and in the next to drop everything in order to get a working wheelchair to a crippled Jewish girl in the middle of nowhere.

אלו ואלו
ELU VE-ELU (PLURALISM)

The Hebrew phrase *elu ve-elu* (literally, "these and those") is taken from the Talmudic phrase regarding legal disputes among various rabbinic schools, "These and those are the words of the living God" (BT *Eruvin* 13b). The Joint works with Jews of every persuasion without regard to denominational preference. It recognizes no differences of color or ethnic origin. Even the halachic definition of a Jew is too restrictive for the Joint. Those in Communist Yugoslavia who saw themselves as Jews and identified with the community were considered as such by the JDC.

The Talmudic quote notwithstanding, twenty–first-century pluralism is hardly an ancient Jewish concept. Its roots are to be found in Rabbinic statements such as "A Jew who sins remains a Jew" (BT *Sanhedrin* 44a), "All of Israel have a share in the World to Come" (BT *Sanhedrin* 90a) and "The Torah has seventy faces [interpretations]" (*Bamidbar Rabbah*, Parashat Naso, 13:15). It is not easy to translate these concepts into a tolerant pluralism that respects diversity. It is even more difficult to operate in the field with diverse Jews of opposing opinions, but that was the ideal for which the JDC strove, even if not always with complete success.

While the organization was devoted primarily to work within the Jewish community, it did not shy away from its wider responsibilities on this planet. There were programs specifically designed for non-sectarian humanitarian aid and, of course, all major natural disasters demanded an early response from the JDC. The Joint's assistance after the Moroccan earthquake in the month of Ramadan, 1960 was a contribution that all Moroccans recognized as coming from the soul of a nation that knows its universal responsibilities.

■ ■ ■ ■ ■

But these are the obvious values of an organization devoted to aid. There were other, more subtle concerns that presented themselves as challenges to the accepted norms. One can never forget the constant prophetic remark by the Joint's patriarch (and my first JDC boss), Ralph Goldman: *"Mi samcha?"* – Who appointed you? From whence comes your authority? This quote comes from Exodus 2:14, in which a fellow Israelite challenges Moses's authority. "Who appointed you chief and ruler over us?"

It wasn't easy having a boss who could correct my Hebrew and quote scripture, but very few of us could ignore this demand for institutional humility. We were working in vastly different communities, each one unique in its historical and geographic context. Nevertheless, they all shared the right to exist, grow, and flourish with freedom. It was far too easy to be patronizing (with the best of intentions) or to apply foreign formulae from other communal realities.

I can remember some of our more dramatic errors in this regard. A country director entering Morocco with Western prejudice could easily favor one of the four school systems (Alliance Israélite Universelle, ORT, Lubavitch and Ozar HaTorah) over the others simply because of the desire to give Moroccan youth an advantage in the countries they were destined to inhabit as adults. While it sounds reasonable, it does not take into account family traditions, Moroccan modes of learning, the personalities involved, and many other factors that only the locals could understand and appreciate fully.

Our field representatives in the FSU were all Russian-speaking Israelis. We did this to put an Israeli face on our operation so that it would be clear that we agreed with both the Israeli government and the Jewish Agency that the first priority for FSU Jews was aliyah. Only those who chose to stay or those who could not leave were our targets for rebuilding community and for reconnecting to Judaism. It was helpful that our field staff spoke both the language of the locals and Hebrew, the *lingua franca* of most foreign workers in the Jewish sphere. The origins of these representatives, however, did pose problems. They were usually former Russians who mostly assumed that while you could take the Jew out of the USSR, you couldn't take the USSR out of the Jew! It was difficult for many of them to identify with the enthusiasm and innocence of the rebirth that surrounded them. Also, they were mostly secular Israelis convinced that the entire Jewish world was divided into the secular and religious categories of Israel. Synagogues were for the religious minority and cemeteries were state concerns. These workers did not easily understand Reform, Orthodox, Conservative, and all the other movements and tendencies of Diaspora Jewry.

I was once waiting for a meeting with a new Jewish teacher from the FSU, while with me was a senior Israeli educator acting as a consultant to our organization. When the FSU educator arrived, he donned a kippah for the meeting. My Israeli colleague scorned this behavior, claiming that the fellow was not religious and only wore the skullcap to impress me (another kippah-wearer). The Israeli reality is one of either religious or secular (at least, on the surface); kippah on *or* off. In the Diaspora, the kippah can be on *and* off. My reading of the same situation was that this educator had only recently learned that Jewish education was a sacred act and that its work required a head covering. In North America, it would be perfectly normal for a Conservative or Reform educator to cover his head at work, but not elsewhere.

One thing I have learned about moral values is that the simple ones are easy to define and defend. Motherhood, apple pie, *tzedaka,* Jewish learning, and *tikkun olam* are all universally understood and promoted. It is the more complex concepts such as *ahavat Yisrael, chesed,* and pluralism that create tension and debate, as do conflicts between normative values. Does an American organization enter Soviet Ukraine in cooperation with a dictator such as Lenin to save starving Jews in the 1920s? What about working with a tyrant like Mengistu in order to be permitted to re-enter Ethiopia in the early 1990s?

Strangely, these latter types of dilemmas were easy to solve compared to those posed within the Jewish community. Can a Jewish organization funded and governed mostly by liberal Jews support religious activities run by an Orthodox body that is patently intolerant of liberal Judaism? The mix of *chesed,* defined as acts of compassion beyond the call of duty, *ahavat Yisrael,* understood to mean acts of unconditional love, and pluralism in its twenty-first century mode creates moral and ethical problems difficult to solve. I found that the tension fomented by these issues as they presented themselves in everyday field situations created a forum for Jewish peoplehood in the host communities, among my JDC colleagues, and within our partner organizations in the field.

The clashes between Ashkenazi and Sephardi, the various religious denominations vying for influence, Israeli and Diaspora organizations, Zionists, non-Zionists, and anti-Zionists, and between an American and a European perspective – all of these challenges to UJA's "We Are One!" slogan became real-time moral decisions in the field operations of the communities where I worked. Profound human and Jewish values were often in conflict, and I was reminded many times that difficult ethical decisions involved cutting off other options.

Moroccan Jews had become accustomed to the fact that they could present themselves at the emergency department of a Paris hospital and receive care. At a certain point, that was no longer possible without giving the hospital a considerable cash advance, but the myth persisted among the poor Jews of Casablanca that, somehow, it would still work. A severely ill woman flew to Paris on her way to aliyah to Israel, but once in Paris, decided to jump ship and to present herself at a local hospital. The original plan was for her to receive medical treatment in Israel immediately after her arrival. When the hospital demanded a huge cash advance, the Jewish social services in Paris and the JDC office both refused. I agreed to the refusal, since the money would have been deducted from a specific budget that dealt with legitimate medical emergencies. The woman died waiting for our decision. We were completely justified in our denial of funding, but neither the relatives nor the Casablanca community understood. The relatives only knew that she was dying and that good French medicine could cure her. The community leaders did not appreciate the budgetary limitations of "Uncle Joint," nor did they value financial planning for future urgencies. Differing perspectives create conflicting values. For a while, some in the community must have seen me as the murderous country director.

However, it was in the area of Jewish communal governance that most conflicts arose and the tension was most palpable. Interestingly, in both North Africa and the FSU, there was a sense among the local Jews that they had considerable control over their communal affairs. In Morocco, this was the case due to centuries of communal self-government under weak central systems and the current kingdom, which granted the community specific domains of jurisdiction. In the FSU, and especially in Siberia, the central and local post-Communist authorities were weak in the early 1990s, but nevertheless asserted the right of ethnic (in Russian parlance, national) entities to re-establish themselves after seven decades of Soviet repression.

As an illustration, in Morocco, all family law is handled by religious courts, and community rabbis who work as judges in those courts are paid by the Ministry of Justice. Also, the taxes on kosher meat and wine are returned to the Jewish community for self-government. In Krasnajarsk, Siberia, one of the first major moves by the local government was to erect a beautiful building on the river to house the offices of all ethnic societies and to give them exhibition and concert space. In many Siberian communities, the Jews were among the first to assert their rights as a religious and cultural entity under the new realities of post-Communist Russia.

This potential for Jewish self-governance, even if it is limited to certain communal domains, sounds idyllic, but in fact, it was always problematic. There were always "the foxes, the little foxes, that spoil the vineyards" to interfere. The reference to the Song of Songs (2:15) is apt for Morocco since that community so revered that particular Biblical text.

By the time I arrived in Morocco, the 1945 population of over three hundred thousand Jews had been reduced to between ten thousand and fifteen thousand. Most of the significant leadership in communal affairs, business, and the rabbinate had already left. By 1981, the former Chief Rabbi of Casablanca was the Sephardic Chief Rabbi of Jerusalem. However, well before the post-1948 exodus external forces had already asserted their influence. The Paris-based Alliance Israélite Universelle had opened its first schools in Morocco in the second half of the nineteenth century, before the French Protectorate. By 1981, all Moroccan Jewish schools were of external origin: Ittihad (Alliance), Lubavitch (Russian Chasidic), Ozar HaTorah (funded originally by a New York Syrian family), and ORT (based in London). However, almost all the teachers and principals were local. One can easily imagine the tensions that existed among these various systems and internally in each of them. What was even more significant was how they managed to function side by side and produce generations of well-versed young Moroccan Jews.

To take the most unlikely match as an example, I was often asked by visitors (especially non-Chasidic rabbis!) how Lubavitch had found itself in a Sephardic community and how the JDC dared fund such an aberration. There were three Lubavitch families in Casablanca during my time. The oldest had been sent in 1950 by the previous Lubavitch Rebbe, Yosef Yitzchak Schneersohn. Since the mass immigration of Iberian Jews into Morocco at the end of the fifteenth century there had been no shifts in population to compare with the mass emigrations after 1948. Lubavitch had shared this challenging period with the remnant of Moroccan Jews, and because of that they had become part of the family. They too remembered having thousands of students, while by 1981, their numbers had been reduced to mere hundreds. It must also be noted that both traditions shared a pre-Enlightenment version of natural, unself-conscious Judaism. The Lubavitch prayer book, being Chasidic and *nusach Sefard,* was closer to the Moroccan rite than Ashkenazi prayer books were, and both Lubavitch and Moroccan folk religion revered the graves of tzaddikim (*des Saints* in French) and conducted pilgrimages to cemeteries on special occasions. Indeed, one of our Lubavitch winter camps was in a well-known cemetery in Ouezzane. Moroccan Jews build vacation huts near their favourite saints' graves in order to pass some time in prayer and meditation, and this particular cemetery had so many huts that we could rent it for a campsite. This was the only Jewish camp I ever attended that was off-limits for kohanim because of the prohibition against priestly families entering a cemetery!

What of the knowledge and concern that Lubavitch brought to *kashrut,* the dietary laws that were equally important to ninety-nine percent of Moroccan Jewish households? It was a Lubavitch emissary who, by 1981, replaced the missing rabbinic leadership that had once supervised such important community functions. This man was equally popular with common Jews who ate meat thanks to him, with the ritual slaughterers and inspectors whom he had trained into a livelihood, and with the lay leadership of the community because of the thousands of dollars in revenue that kosher meat and wine produced for the community.

There are many examples, which will be told later in this book, of the intricate relationships among the various schools, community organs, and the JDC, which was alone in Morocco as a representative of world Jewry. Suffice it to say that all of these complex dynamics had their potential for conflict and tension. Sometimes those tensions were overwhelming and caused communal strife, while other times the problems would be resolved in ways that give us hope for a Jewish peoplehood that, if not unified, can at least channel its diversity into growth and development.

To digress for a moment, the historical example of this kind of creative unity in diversity that I favor is the codification of the Mishna in the third century C.E. While it is clear from the text of the Mishna itself that there were divergent views on many areas of Jewish law and practice, the spiritual masters of that period creatively and jointly decided to break with earlier custom (not Jewish continuity, this!) and to write down what had been previously preserved as an oral tradition. In doing this they not only exacerbated the divisions among themselves, but they also created a new institution of legal codification which was both a model to all of western civilization and a pillar of all Jewish life to come.

There is some element of mystery in the way that Jewish innovation and creativity can emerge from the tensions of peoplehood. I take that to be the central theme of this book and believe it to be the force that binds most of my stories to one another.

I had two sets of overlapping duties in the FSU in the 1990s. By 1991 I was named the director of Jewish education for all JDC operations, but I also had area director responsibilities in Siberia, which meant that in Siberia I supervised all JDC areas of concern, while in the rest of the FSU my staff and I concerned ourselves with all the emerging forms of Jewish education. Since my concerns in Siberia were community-wide and because of the affection and respect I developed for the warm Jews of this cold clime, it is in the vastness of this territory that I will cite mysteries similar to those in Morocco regarding communal tension and maturing growth.

In Psalm 137 we are given a moving description of the early days of the Babylonian captivity in the sixth century B.C.E. The captives, having already hung up their musical instruments, no longer capable of music, are urged to sing a song of Zion. They reply that they cannot sing God's song in a foreign land. The identification of Zion with God points to the early trauma of abandonment that they felt in those first days of exile. God stayed behind in Jerusalem, and they were devastatingly alone. It is only in memory that they can exist as a people. "If I forget thee, O Jerusalem, let my right hand forget its cunning." The Jews of Morocco had centuries to develop their theology so that God was very much with them, even in the far west of the Maghreb. But the Jews of Siberia had lost that God of memory and were living in a Godless state by the time Communism fell.

On my first visit to Khabarovsk in the far east of Russia, I found a community of several thousand Jews who had just been given license to redefine themselves as a religion, an ethnic entity, a nation in the old Soviet nomenclature, a language – all or any of the above. There is a legend about a dissident Soviet Jew who was given permission to fly to England and wrote in the UK immigration form that his nationality was Jewish. The officer at the airport corrected him by stating that his nationality must be Russian. He answered by asking who knew better who he was. "You are telling me who I am?" As confused as our new Jews in Khabarovsk were, they immediately broke into two organizations: Mizrach, a "religious" group demanding synagogue property and such things, and Shalom, a cultural organ seeking ethnic identity. From the moment I encountered these Jews and their divisions, I knew that they had not completely lost their memory and that they were well on their way to taking their rightful place in our tiny people.

Of course, in the FSU, the Joint was not alone as a Jewish helping organization, as we were in Morocco. I recall a funny incident in Cheliabinsk of the Urals when I was invited to visit the Beitar club. On arrival I noticed many pictures of the Lubavitcher Rebbe and a great deal of Messiah agitprop. When I asked the obvious question, I was duly informed that Chabad had paid the rent until the previous month, but now Beitar was footing the bill. A knowing smile accompanied the answer. Once again, I was reassured that I was dealing with non-innocents. Once in St. Petersburg, I heard a local educator berate the Jewish Agency emissary by stating that he knew what other Diaspora communities thought of the Agency, but that here in this new community they had no choice but to accept the patronizing that accompanied funding. We in the JDC were told many times that we were the least offensive of a bad lot of condescending outsiders.

I remember my first visit to Irkutsk when my translator (French this time, due to a dearth of English speakers in mid-Siberia) told me that she was getting very bad vibes from the president of the community in my presence. The "community" was all of a few months old, but whatever I proposed, he rejected. "Should I send a library of Jewish books in translation?" "No." "Would you like us to organize a Passover Seder for the city?" "No." After some complex research, I discovered that he saw himself as a Zionist and had heard that the Joint was an anti-Zionist organization determined to keep the Jews in Irkutsk. I needed to get my new friends from communities all over the Russian territory to speak to him on my behalf before he would trust me to assist him in his work. We soon became good friends and he later made aliyah, as did most of our community leaders. In fact, in those early years, most of the first and second waves of community leadership left for Israel, which is what we expected and hoped for. Once most of those Jews came to the center of their respective communities and became better grounded in their Jewishness, they came to see their place elsewhere, mostly in Israel.

In a full chapter devoted to education I will chronicle the educational activity in both North Africa and the FSU. Here, too, there were difficult decisions to be made based on the local culture, the historical moment, and the ubiquitous limitations of budget. The director of the Ozar HaTorah schools in Morocco would point to a building at the Neve Chalom site and remark that the JDC opposed its being built in the 1960s. The thinking was that the community had little time left and that a capital investment in infrastructure made no sense. Rabbi Monsonego could not easily define what a capital investment in infrastructure was, but he knew that, since the 1960s, generations of young people received their primary and secondary education in that building and then went on to build their lives elsewhere, with the wealth of Moroccan Jewish custom and lore that Ozar HaTorah provided.

I once asked a teacher-emissary from Israel what she hoped to accomplish in her first months of teaching in the Stockholm Jewish school. She wanted to teach them how to properly celebrate Hanukah. When I asked her where she lived in Israel, she gave me the name of a settlement that was about twenty years old. I needed to know if she knew how many centuries Jews have been celebrating Hanukah in Sweden!

While we might have guessed how distant FSU Jews would be from their Jewish literary, cultural, and spiritual sources after seventy years of Communism, we grossly underestimated both the thirst for that knowledge and the speed with which these Jews would organize structures and programs to quench that thirst. Of course, every foreign group offering assistance had its own agenda. The denominations hoped for loyalty to and membership in their respective groupings: Chabad, Reform, religious Zionist, Conservative, and so on. At first the Jewish Agency rejected all educational activity except Hebrew-language ulpanim, since, in their view, everyone was leaving that year. The Government of Israel, as represented by the Liaison Bureau, wanted to create Israeli transition schools to prepare children for entry into the Israeli system. The JDC saw schools as part of a larger community structure in the making. Even before the USSR disintegrated, the locals started adult Hebrew classes, opened Sunday schools where the entire family could study, requested space in municipal pre-schools for Jewish programs, began experimental day schools, and initiated academic Jewish studies on campus. They had only one agenda: the forbidden fruit of the Soviet era, Jewish knowledge.

It was as if a secret had been passed along from the grandparents of the Czarist period to the great-grandchildren of the late 1980s that Jewish study would reconnect this lost limb to the corpus of the Jewish people. If one could forget the individual mission of any foreign group and just observe the frenzy of activity in 1989, 1990, and 1991, one would be in what Abraham Joshua Heschel termed "radical amazement." Elie Wiesel's "Jews of Silence" were making cosmic noise, many decibels louder than any of us had imagined.

We were dealing with a mass of ignorance unparalleled in our history, with vestigial stigmas produced by years of persecution, and with a heterogeneous mix spread over eleven time zones. To counter that, we had intellectual curiosity, the adaptability of the Soviet citizen, and a mysterious quality—the Jewish spark, which had been almost but not quite extinguished. One story from Khabarovsk sums it up.

Whenever possible, we preceded our first trip to a community with a shipment of Jewish and Zionist books in Russian in order to form the kernel of a community library. In the early days, we were never quite certain whether the books had arrived, we got them to the right person, or they would end up anywhere but in some private cupboard. On my first trip to Khabarovsk I was the guest at a luncheon in the apartment of the leader of Mizrach, the first Jewish organization in town. A local English teacher had taught herself enough Hebrew to be the first Sunday school teacher and the most knowledgeable Jew around. She asked to make a toast (a Russian custom we soon got to know and love) and in doing so, thanked me and the Joint for the books we sent. (Whew! They'd arrived.) She pointed out that Khabarovsk, unlike Moscow or Kiev, had had no access to Jewish books in the dark years. There were no *samizdat* copies of *Exodus* being passed from home to home. The few volumes we had sent were the very first pieces of Jewish heritage to reach the banks of the Amur River.

Yet our teacher had a question. She noted that we had sent the book that Jews use in their churches. "Synagogues," I corrected. Hidden in that volume was another small book, only six chapters, that could not by any means be Jewish in origin. I explained that we no longer hid books and I could not understand what she meant. "This little book is too humane, too noble to be Jewish. It must be a Christian book." It took some time to figure out that she was talking about *Pirkei Avot,* the section of the Mishna called *Ethics of the Fathers,* inserted in most traditional prayer books after the Shabbat afternoon service, and read a chapter per week during the summer months. Indeed, a noble piece of our heritage, but written by authentic Jews!

When we tried to imagine the Jews we would encounter on our first trips, we must have thought of the few hundred dissidents and refuseniks that we knew from the 1970s and 1980s, their names still symbols of that movement's courage. In truth, however, the great masses of Jews were mostly interested in distancing themselves from the stigma of a Jewish name or the classification "Jew" in an internal Soviet passport. The real miracle in the post-Soviet period is the rapidity with which Jews lost the stigma, became lovers of Zion, learned Hebrew, and reconnected to the Jewish people.

One of the strange ironies of the latter half of the twentieth century is that while much of North African Jewish culture and spirituality were lost to the assimilating forces of secular France, Quebec, and Israel, at the very end of the century, a huge disabled sector of the Jewish people reconnected to its land, language, religion, and culture; rapidly gaining back the faculties destroyed by the Soviet regime. Is this the kind of oversimplified generalization that twists the truth into a facile collection of falsehoods and misconceptions? I think not.

While much remains of Moroccan Jewish culture in Jerusalem, Ashdod, Netivot, Paris, Nice, and Montreal, much was also lost to the acculturation required by the secular, socialist regime of 1950s Israel, by French society and citizenship, and to the freedom of the Canadian mosaic of cultures. How ironic that this ancient culture was not permitted to flourish in societies supposedly designed for freedom and equality.

While this is not the place to examine the particular qualities of the host and guest cultures that prevented such development, here too there are mysteries to unravel.

My favorite story of this sad loss is one told by an Israeli colleague, a high school teacher in the 1960s. He tells of a class trip to the Galilee region, which stopped at a ruin of an ancient synagogue. Some of the Moroccan students in this secular high school (how the categories defeat us!) decided that it was fitting to hold the afternoon service, *mincha*, at a synagogue ruin. Some donned kippot, others used pocket handkerchiefs to cover their heads, and they began to recite a worship service that was in their very genes. (That feat alone, praying by heart, is not possible for the overwhelming majority of Jews who now inhabit the earth!) My colleague overheard the scornful remarks of their teachers: "After all we have done for them, they still remain primitives."

I am not one of those who lay all the blame for the cultural and spiritual losses of this period on the misguided teachers and social workers of the Labor establishment of early Israel. There were forces at play within some ancient cultures that made them difficult to transport and relocate, and there were legitimate modern tendencies in western civilization that militated against ethnic divisions and old-time religion. (There are lots of *tefillin* in the waters around Ellis Island!) Nevertheless, we should note the paradox of open societies that were not as open as we might have hoped.

Even in the mass movement of FSU immigrants to Israel in the 1990s, many mistakes were made, but the numbers alone illustrate the enormity of the challenge that both Israel and certain Diaspora communities faced. By the time the total number of *olim* had reached seven hundred thousand, a *New Yorker* article compared that figure (which soon reached one million) to the equivalent of the United States settling the combined populations of Canada and Australia. This *aliyah*, with all its problems, was part of a larger process for the Jewish people, unlike anything that had come before. This was the complex return of the

Jews of the Soviet regime from the technocratic, totalitarian, secular state that was the USSR to a new reality in Israel, the FSU, Germany, North America, and other places where they could flourish or disappear culturally, ethnically, spiritually, and linguistically – as they wished. Who would have guessed that the new Hebrew grammar experts of twenty-first century Israeli universities would be transplanted Russians? Could there be hundreds of Jewish schools and dozens of universities teaching Jewish studies in the former territory of the Soviet Union? The phenomenon of FSU immigrants in united Germany, transforming a tiny Jewish population into one of the strongest post-1945 European Jewish communities, could never have been predicted. They cannot ever be Germans, nor do they dare to be Russians in post-Berlin Wall Germany, so they end up being Jews, and many of them are identifying positively with their new Diaspora status.

To return to my question of whether these gross generalizations hide the many exceptions that exist alongside the mainstream of these well-documented tendencies, I must clarify that it is precisely the exceptions that illustrate the point. North African Jewish culture thrives in synagogues around the world, in the dozens of kosher restaurants of Paris, and still somewhat in Casablanca, but it was dealt a blow by the open culture of the latter half of the twentieth century that severely altered its place in the mosaic of Jewish life. To be fair, while many post-Soviet Jews are still very distant from full identification with Jewish values and history (Russian ghettos exist equally in Karmiel, Berlin, and Brighton Beach!), the reattachment of the limb of FSU Jews to the body of the Jewish people will definitively change the family of Jews in this new century.

I wander back to the questions I posed at the beginning of this introduction. What connects these stories and what lessons do we learn from them? The answer may be found within the question. As much as I gave of myself during my eighteen years of JDC fieldwork, I gained much more. In "doing" Jewish history, I grew and developed my own concepts of the family of Jews in the differing contexts of the communities I served. What connects these stories to each other, to me, and to the Jewish world are the very lessons I learned in the realm of pluralism and creative growth.

I came to understand that twenty-first century Jewish pluralism is much more complex and complicated in practice than in its theoretical imperatives. While we expect certain fundamentalist forces to reject even the language of pluralism, we find that liberal movements at the other end of the spectrum can be just as guilty of the sin of exclusion, even as both proclaim their adherence to the principle of *ahavat Yisrael*, the love of the Jewish people.

Just as telling is the weak chord that the sloganism of Jewish continuity and survival strikes in my soul. So many of the stories are testimony to the fact that proud and courageous Jews aspire to creative growth and a flourishing future rather than mere survival and continuity of the past. Here, too, devotion to survival reduces Jewish life to an energy-consuming struggle, while dedication to growth and development has the potential for a photosynthesis of the soul, producing blossoms and fruit.

In the stories that follow, the reader will find the lessons I discovered and, I hope, many more.

CHAPTER ONE

FIRST ENCOUNTERS

WHEN I THINK BACK TO my first days in Casablanca in 1981, my memory corresponds well with the notes in my field journal. In researching this book, I found that this was not always the case. I had been given good advice to keep a field journal and managed to leave the JDC in 1999 writing in volume 43, but human memory often twists the past in strange ways.

I think that those first weeks of August and September 1981 were so new and challenging that the memories were etched deeply into my mind. However, there was one incident of a previous trip that set the tone for much of what I experienced during my North African period. In the spring of 1981 the JDC sent me for a one-week visit to Casablanca to see whether the Joint, Morocco, and Epstein were all suited to each other. Most of what I remember from that brief trip was the surface exotica of North African culture (I hadn't really seen anything yet!), but one incident remained with me forever.

As I was leaving my hotel on the last day, the porter asked me if I was Jewish. Nervous as I was about my status in an Arab country, I admitted my religion with some hesitation. He then told me that the saddest day in Moroccan history was when the Jews decided to leave en masse.

That incident became the first of many discoveries of the deep Jewish roots in Morocco. No history book could have so etched the Jewish motifs of Morocco in my consciousness as did the many moments that made this Ashkenazi, western Jew feel so at home in the Maghreb.

When I arrived in the late summer of 1981, the JDC office felt I would appreciate living on the beach until I found an apartment. The modest hotel I inhabited was owned by a Jew, and I soon learned that although the large city of Casablanca was inhabited by millions of Muslims, the tiny Jewish community (perhaps as many as 15,000 in 1981) saw the Atlantic corniche as their special place of refuge from the city heat. There were favorite "Jewish" beaches, hotels famous for their hospitality to Jews, and even a kosher beach restaurant.

The day after Rosh ha-Shana 5742 in 1981, I was shopping for some fabric in a Casablanca street market. My maid had decided to sew me a new tablecloth and told me where to buy the material. The Arab merchant asked if I was Jewish. This time, with somewhat more confidence, I replied in the affirmative, and he immediately asked me if I was fasting. While the overwhelming majority of Jews in North America don't know that the day after Rosh ha-Shana, Tzom Gedalya, is a fast day, this Muslim in North Africa, who had lived and worked with traditional Jews for decades, knew the custom well.

Of course, not all my experiences in Morocco were positive. I was accosted twice in Fes with anti-Semitic curses and was told of street altercations that gave one reason for concern. The foreign policy of the King and his government was overtly anti-Zionist, and the younger generation had come under the influence of pan-Arab nationalism, Muslim fundamentalism, and its concomitant anti-Israel militancy. Yet the government went to great lengths to demonstrate both its respect for the Jewish past of the country and its ongoing philo-Semitism. The most prominent illustration of that is the Hebrew date on the masthead of a government-controlled daily newspaper!

One last African story sums up the warmth I usually felt as a vestige of a past of sincere coexistence. My wife and I were spending a few days of vacation in the southern tourist town of Agadir during Ramadan. We had gone to a local café for morning coffee, the understanding being that non-Muslim tourists could eat publicly during Ramadan in liberal Morocco. While the writer was happy to serve blonde Cheryl, he was convinced that I was a Moroccan living abroad who had come back home on vacation and refused to serve me. My protest of being a Canadian did not help. For him, my current passport had no significance. I then had to decide between *Nasrani* (Christian) or *Yahudi* (Jew) to get my coffee. Totally confident by 1987, I promptly announced *"Ana Yahudi"* and received a broad smile, coffee, orange juice, and everything else I wanted!

In contrast, I think back to the first Vaad meeting in Moscow in 1989. There was a small delegation of JDC senior staff who were the pioneers of our Soviet program. We were there because *glasnost* and *perestroika* had permitted the Soviet Communists enough liberalism to invite the JDC back, cautiously, into the USSR. The same late-1980s openness had prompted the Jews of some major cities to organize themselves into a *vaad* (council in English, *soviet* in Russian) representing the Jews of the various Soviet republics. Unlike Casablanca and Morocco, Moscow and Russia had never been overly hospitable to Jews. Indeed, the past seventy years of Communism had seen decades of edicts that distanced Jews from their religion, their languages, their values, and their literature.

The lingering pride I witnessed among the few remaining Jews of Morocco was in sharp contrast to the stigma that Soviet Jews felt. I sensed that Jews throughout the Soviet Union of 1989 literally identified with the Israelite slaves in Egypt who saw themselves as repugnant in the eyes of their masters. They had been told for so long that they were parasites and pariah that they began to believe it themselves. But in December 1989 we were boldly venturing into this strange planet, conscious of the gravity of the historical moment (the why of it all), but totally ignorant of what, how, and when.

On the cold morning that the conference began, we had some difficulty finding transportation in a van for the six of us who were attending. Since we were determined to stay together at all times, we reluctantly hired the white stretch Cadillac limousine that the hotel insisted was the only large car available. Intent on keeping a low profile in the JDC style, we got out of the limousine two blocks before the conference building and were walking the last bit of the way when we noticed some sort of reception committee greeting the conference delegates at the door. It wasn't until we got very close and our one Russian speaker could read the placards that we realized that this was not a reception but rather a protest from some local anti-Semitic group. A snowball hurled in anger at one of our members made this abundantly clear in a few fearful moments.

That day defined for me one of the major differences between my fascinating years in an ancient, once-great, disintegrating community and the challenging time to come in a lost community that was soon to rediscover itself. While North Africa certainly had its sad Jewish moments, the overwhelming beauty of its proud heritage had clearly become the motif of its centuries of coexistence with its Muslim neighbors. While Russian Jews had had their golden moments and contributed greatly to much of contemporary Jewish and Israeli life, so much of what they were in 1989 had been profoundly poisoned by Russian folk anti-Semitism and the anti-Jewish persecutions of the Soviet regime.

In Morocco, mostly the past was glorious, while in the USSR only the future could give us hope.

CHAPTER TWO

EDUCATION

SINCE JEWISH EDUCATION is my career and since most of my work in the JDC was connected to some aspect of it, a large part of this book deals with the issues surrounding education in the countries where I worked. I should point out that while my first posting with the JDC was as a pedagogic consultant in Morocco, it was made clear to me that if I wanted to stay on after the first two years of contract work, I would have to become a "generalist." In order to work as a country director, I needed to acquire skills and experience in the other areas of JDC concern; community organization, welfare, health, care for the aged, and so on.

After re-reading some articles and a memorandum written during my years of service – which I have appended to the end of this chapter – I think back to my original position in Casablanca, where I was sent as a pedagogic consultant on a two-year contract. As happens in these situations, everyone had a different idea of what my job should be. The JDC headquarters had a particular sense of what the posting entailed, the JDC country director in Morocco was hoping for an assistant and, ultimately, a replacement, the locals had their own different notion of my role, and I slowly developed still another definition of my responsibilities to the Jewish children and teachers of Morocco. It was the discrepancy between my own sense of the job and that of the local educators that made me the most uneasy.

While I preferred that I be introduced as a *conseiller pedagogique*, invariably I would be referred to as *Monsieur l'inspecteur*. I quickly came to understand their need for an inspector to test the levels of Jewish knowledge of the children. Previous outsiders sent by the JDC and the Alliance Israélite had done just that, and since the French system demanded formal inspections in general studies, the local educators were only too happy for me to serve a parallel function in Hebrew and Jewish studies. This would have limited my role to entering classrooms, asking selected questions in various subjects such as Hebrew language, Bible, and Jewish law, and leaving with either a frown or a smile.

Of course, I wanted to deal with the quality of teaching, not merely with the quantity of material learned. For me, this meant following the observation patterns I knew from my years of training teachers at McGill University. I wanted to sit quietly at the back of the class for a considerable time, observe a routine class, and take notes. My idea was to then follow up with individual conversations with teachers and principals and offer corrective in-service training where necessary.

As it turned out, however, the job of *Monsieur l'inspecteur* was to stand at the head of the class and ask questions of children whom he didn't know. If the teacher taught at all, it was to put on a show, not to actually teach a normal lesson. In addition, my note-taking made everyone in an oral-aural culture quite nervous. I could only be writing terrible things that I intended to share with others.

Every classroom observer fears the show class of what we in Jewish education came to call *hazerai*, a Yiddish pun on *hazara* (review) that blends the prohibition against eating pork (*hazir*) with the re-teaching of material that the children already know by heart. There was even a trick I learned as a novice teacher to deceive the odd inspector who might arrive. One instructed the students to all raise their hands for every question asked. If they were certain they had the right answer, they were to raise their right hand, and if not, their left. This ensured full participation, awe on the part of the inspector who dutifully noted that every student seemed conversant with the material, and total shock that every answer was correct!

So even though I knew all the pitfalls and tricks, I never managed to convince the local headmasters that all I wanted to do was observe and help. This difference in perspective became all the more problematic once I had identified certain areas which I thought required intervention.

The first such area was corporal punishment. I had observed some pushing of children and a bit of hitting, but waited until I had a larger view of the culture before I decided to speak out. Just as I was deciding that this mild form of aggression might be part of the cultural landscape and not worth opposing, I started to receive some complaints from parents. Although that gave me pause, I still wondered whether those very parents did not hit their children occasionally themselves and only wanted to make sure that the teachers refrained from doing so without parental consent. Then I observed something in a school lunchroom that convinced me to act. A teacher had left his stick (the presence of which I was already sadly used to) on a table when a young girl picked it up and imitated the teacher by randomly hitting several children nearby.

I decided to devote one of my sessions with the teachers to the topic of corporal punishment. How could I convince them? I gave up on the idea of quoting Talmudic sources opposed to it since I knew that several teachers would be able to quote other Talmudic passages that supported it. After the session, all I remembered was being listened to politely and mostly ignored. However, the next day one of the teachers came to my office to explain that he agreed with me that hitting a child was an improper technique for punishment of discipline problems. He only used the stick to reinforce learning! That was one of those moments when I realized that there really are different universes of discourse.

While that particular argument did not convince me, there were times when my assessment of Moroccan teaching technique led me to search for corrective measures at first, but later caused me to question some of my own assumptions based on North American practice. I remember observing several classes before deciding that I had to change three things in the teaching of Hebrew. One was a detail of enunciation that had nothing to do with Sephardic pronunciation; it was just an error that most of the first-grade teachers were making. I made absolutely no progress on that one. The next was the use of *Monsieur* or *Madame* to address teachers. I felt that *Moreh* or *Morah* would be better, and made some progress. Finally, there was the general use of Hebrew terms. I wanted the teachers who spoke French to their students to introduce more Hebrew, and I felt that the use of certain terms such as *luach* for blackboard, *gir* for chalk, *todah* for thank you, and so on, would gradually change the environment. I knew that some of the teachers might find it difficult to use entire grammatical constructs and thought that the use of key words was a fair compromise. Again, some progress.

In reflecting on this issue, however, I came to re-think the use of Hebrew in North American day schools. At the time, there was already a debate about the use of full Hebrew instruction (what was called *ivrit be-ivrit*) versus the freedom that children need to express themselves in their first language. No school in North America had dared to institute full Hebrew immersion, as was done in pre-war Poland, when both general and Jewish subjects were taught in Hebrew. Interestingly enough, the only Diaspora school that I know of that uses full Hebrew immersion is Torah v' Chinuch on the island of Djerba. But many day schools were teaching all Jewish subject matter in Hebrew and experiencing difficulty regarding the students' ability to express themselves freely, especially in upper grades. Did the use of Hebrew stifle important questions and limit answers to formulaic, one-word responses?

Of course, a major difference was the use of indigenous teachers in Morocco versus the Israeli teachers who work in many North American day schools. The advantages of an indigenous teacher far outweigh most other considerations. While the Moroccan teachers had little training and were not native speakers of Hebrew, their commonality of milieu with their students was their greatest asset. They came from the same streets, learned in the same seats, and prayed in the same synagogues as their charges. They knew and enjoyed the same sports and they ate exactly the same food in their culture of conservative palates. When I was in elementary school in the 1950s, my teachers were either Israelis or Holocaust survivors, neither of whom liked hockey or pizza.

A Chumash class taught in French by a teacher who lives on your street, who uses only a Hebrew text and conversation filled with Hebrew verbs and nouns, is probably a better locus for real education than one taught completely in Hebrew by a stranger.

This issue of indigenous teachers versus *shlichim* (emissaries from Israel) became a serious concern in the FSU soon after schools started to open in 1990. The Israeli Ministry of Education and the Jewish Agency were happy to send trained teachers to the new schools that were opening up in virtually every FSU city, and in many communities, these teachers were critical to the schools' success. However, early on it became clear that foreign teachers did not meet the needs of this particular population. Many of them were not trained to teach Hebrew, but were teachers who merely happened to speak Hebrew. Because of their secular origins, most of them knew very little about Judaism and classical Jewish sources. Very few of them spoke any Russian or had any real appreciation for Russian culture.

At the very beginning of the Jewish adventure in the USSR, certain local leaders who had a background in education voiced the need for indigenous teachers. In St. Petersburg especially, there were local educators who were re-training themselves to teach Hebrew and Jewish studies, but also thinking in larger terms about what post-Soviet Jewish education should look like. Some of the education conferences run by those St. Petersburg educators were the most inspiring and imaginative I had ever attended.

Observing classes taught by shlichim on the one hand and by local teachers on the other was the key to seeing the full advantage of indigenous instructors. One of the most important aspects was that of modeling. A child could be easily inspired by locals who shared the same love for soccer and chess, knew Russian idiom and who had also decided to renew themselves as Jews. While one could appreciate the effort and sacrifice that the Israeli teachers made in moving to a remote Siberian city for several months, they shared no common roots with their pupils.

The curricular test proved it for me. When the idea of integration of Jewish and general subject matter was introduced, the Russians supported it immediately and began to express themselves creatively in this domain. Integrating Jewish and general studies was a little like reading Marx and Lenin into a Soviet curriculum. Once the local educators realized that they could copy the same technique that they had used all their lives, but apply it to sacred texts, Jewish values, or the Hebrew calendar, they became enthusiastic about the process and began to imagine new curricula.

When such ideas were suggested to the Israelis, however, they were indifferent at the very least. One of the stories written in Russian for a children's book on Jewish holidays had a Chanukah scene on a Russian battlefield during World War II with Jewish soldiers finding each other, lighting candles, and eating potato latkes. I remember representatives of the Israeli educational establishment rejecting the story and not understanding why the characters were Jewish soldiers of the Red Army.

An immediate result of the obvious need for indigenous talent was the development of institutes for Jewish education in various large cities, journals for Jewish educators, teacher-training schools, and the Melton program at Hebrew University. In the mid-1990s, *Ivreiski Shkola* (The Jewish School, after a nineteenth-century Russian Jewish education journal of the same name) was probably the best Jewish education journal in the world. By the end of the 1990s, the Melton Program had brought dozens of FSU educators to Jerusalem for two periods of intensive training and returned them to communities across the FSU to run educational institutions of all kinds. At the same time, the teacher-training seminary in Dnieperpetrovsk was graduating scores of teachers every year, more than all of North America was producing in its few training schools.

I was personally involved in these two programs, which were major sources of satisfaction and pride. The Melton Centre for Jewish Education at Hebrew University trained dozens of educators over several years. The partnership of the JDC, the Jewish Agency, and the Hebrew University helped to make the dream a reality. Another major program of the JDC was the publication of specific texts in Russian in order to provide the new schools with new, post-Soviet curricular materials. (We often referred to our work in this domain as providing color photography instead of black and white.) The purpose of these new works, such as our Scroll of Esther, The Animated Haggadah for Passover, our book about Shabbat and its sequel on the holidays was to give Jewish children an introduction to Jewish traditions that would stay with them for the rest of their lives. Two excerpts from those works (pictured opposite) will illustrate our intentions.[1]

Returning to North Africa, one of the aspects of classroom life that most disturbed me was the children's passivity. The old saw "Children must be seen and not heard" kept going through my head as I sat through hours of frontal teaching with not one single question or comment from a child. One classroom I frequented even had a sign in Hebrew that read, "No Talking in Class." While I knew that this was a prohibition against disturbances and illicit conversations among good

---

[1] We wish to thank Scopus Films/Lambda Publishers, the original publisher of both *The Shabbat Book* and *The Animated Jewish Year,* for their kind permission to reprint the forewords of both books here.

Introducing the Shabbat Book

There are two important differences between the Jewish calendar and those of the general communities. We name our weeks, not our days; the Gregorian calendar names the days and not the weeks. The Hebrew week is divided into six numbered days leading to the seventh and only day with a name – Shabbat. Each week is named after its *Parashat Hashavua*, that week's Torah portion.

This book is dedicated to the idea that a Jew has the capacity to live in Jewish time – Sunday for the Jew becomes *Yom Rishon*, the first of the days leading to Shabbat. The week itself becomes *Breishit*, the first portion of the Torah, or *Mishpatim*, the eighteenth portion and so on. **The Shabbat Book**, in both form and content, teaches us that a Jew looks forward to and prepares for Shabbat all week. During the week a Jew carries with him the narrative, ideas, *mitzvot* and emotions of that week's Torah portion. Over the centuries throughout the world, Shabbat in all its glory and the multi-faceted teachings of the Torah have influenced the lives of individual Jews, their families and their communities.

We hope that as children study the content of a Torah portion each week, along with something new about Shabbat, the influence of these two great Jewish institutions, Shabbat and Torah, will be cultivated in a new generation of Jews.

Dr. Seymour Epstein
Director of Jewish Education,
American Jewish Joint Distribution Committee

1   A special idea found in the text

2   The transliterated name of the book of the Bible which contains this parasha

3   The transliterated name of the week's parasha with its Hebrew equivalent

4   An overview of highlights from the parasha

5   A Shabbat prayer, custom, thought or tale

6   The page number; the season in which we read this parasha

7   Original Hebrew corresponding to the italicized English translation in the text

Seymour Epstein's introduction to
The Shabbat Book.

Introduction

If the previous volume, The Shabbat Book, was meant to introduce Jewish children to Jewish time, this book is designed to explore that time in all of its historical, cultural, ethical, literary and spiritual elements.

The first steps were taken by introducing the Jewish week, in which the Torah portion provides us with a weekly narrative of legend and law, that culminates in the glorious palace we call Shabbat.

Now, in this book, we chart the entire calendar to provide the knowledge, feelings, and internal thoughts surrounding each and every holy day of the Jewish year. The ultimate goal of this book is to put aside the months we know best, January through December, and to learn the rhythm of our own Hebrew months, Tishrei through Elul.

Chaim Nachman Bialik, the national Jewish poet of this century, once wrote an essay to justify the celebration of Chanukah as a national event, aside from any spiritual significance the holiday has for believing Jews. In that brief essay, he uses a metaphor for the holidays of Israel with which all Jews can identify. He compares our holidays, happy and sad, to mountains in time that testify to earlier volcanic eruptions and earthquakes in our history. These were cataclysmic events so powerful at the time that they left indelible records in the annals of our people. As we traverse these "mountains" each year they bring us back to earlier events in our formative years as a people. On the way, we note lesser hills that testify to other dramatic moments in our history, similar in nature and just as significant for those who lived the actual experience.

Since Bialik's writing, we have written new chapters in our history and set aside special days to commemorate these events as well. The generations of the future will see new mountains, where we actually lived the horrors of the Holocaust, the pride of the establishment of the State of Israel, the tragic loss of Israeli soldiers, and the joy of the reunification of Jerusalem, our capital. Yom HaSho'ah VehaGevurah, Yom Ha'Atzma'ut, Yom HaZikaron, and Yom Yerushalayim are, by now, part of our calendar landscape.

This book is dedicated to the "new Jews" of the Former Soviet Union who have come back to the Jewish people after a long spiritual separation. The Russian edition was written for their children in a language they can understand so that, eventually, our holidays will be theirs and our language theirs: our customs of joy and suffering shared by Jews equally all over the world.

Dr. Seymour Epstein
Director of Jewish Education
American Jewish Joint Distribution Committee

Seymour Epstein's introduction to
The Animated Jewish Year.

A young pupil using one of the JDC books.

buddies, I saw it as a metaphor for classrooms where teachers never stopped talking and children never said a word.

The questions asked in class were always ones of rote and ritual, not real questions with answers that require thought and discernment. I longed for a student to challenge an assumption or to ask a question never asked before. Of course, I hoped some teacher would surprise me one day with a query she had never heard before, but what I saw was a classroom ritual that had been played out for several generations. "Who said this to whom?" "Moshe said that to God, Monsieur." "And when did this happen?" "While Moshe was on the mountain, Madame." Just once I wanted to hear, "Why did this happen?," and receive not a memorized answer from the Middle Ages, but one from the imagination of a thinking, feeling child.

While I was impressed that the more talented children managed to learn long passages of Biblical text by heart and that many could quote full commentaries and *midrashim*, I was never certain that any of this knowledge was internalized, and I ached for a critical question or comment. I was also concerned about the few who never answered even the simplest rote questions.

Soon after my classroom observations began, I started to note taller children in several classes. There were a few children in every school who were clearly older than the rest of the class. I began to identify children who were stuck in one place and not learning at all. Some of them were just a bit slower, but making some progress, while others were completely illiterate, not having learned anything in several years of sitting in an elementary school classroom. With a little probing, I became aware of several other children who never made it to school and who spent their entire time at home doing nothing.

Thus began my project to establish a special class for these children. Convinced that the various schools would only continue to babysit them and not offer any special help, I wanted to set up a class in one of the schools, transfer several children to this class, and find an appropriate teacher. No one in the community had any special-education training and the Moroccan public schools had no such programs. I eventually found a local mother who had a kind disposition, some knowledge of Hebrew from a brief sojourn in Israel, and a decent command of French. Her job was defined as ninety percent love and ten percent teaching. The children had few skills, a terribly low self-image, and no reason to trust anyone.

There was a degree of success for a few years and some of the children were even mainstreamed back into regular classes. Nevertheless, one case stands out in my mind. One young boy had no reading or writing skills at all. His French vocabulary was limited to very few words, and he was both sad and a constant source of disturbance in the class. We decided that he had to see himself learn one single thing successfully. As I have mentioned elsewhere, the entire book of *Song of Songs* is read in Moroccan synagogues Friday night as part of the Shabbat welcoming services. In many synagogues, each chapter is read by a different boy, and it was determined that somehow we would train our problem student to recite a full chapter. This involved his learning to read the Hebrew (or memorize it, as appropriate for the oral-aural culture of Morocco) and to learn the liturgical melody. While I never did find out if he actually learned to read the text or if he memorized the entire chapter, I was present the first time that he sang it, and I will never forget the joy in his face and the pride in everyone's heart as he chanted the ancient text perfectly and in tune.

The FSU also presented some pedagogic challenges, since the methods developed over the Soviet years were quite different than those I studied and used. First, Marxist-Leninist doctrine pervaded all curricula except for that of early childhood. As one would expect, the systems were quite rigid, centrally controlled, and not encouraging of independent thought. That said, children in many settings were happy. They learned much more content than their counterparts in western democracies, and many of them had a full menu of extra-curricular activities that included music, sports, chess, ballet, and the plastic arts. By the time I was exposed to FSU education, my approach was relativistic enough to tolerate whatever differences I noted. Children were learning and their teachers were curious enough to ask about the outside world of education.

On several occasions, the locals asked me to give a class on what they called "democratic education." By this term they did not mean teaching democracy (thank God, because I wasn't sure how much of a democrat I was after all those years in the kingdom of Morocco!), but rather progressive pedagogics which stressed open-ended questions and autonomous thinking. I was happy to comply and prepared several sessions on a variety of topics. However, when I asked for the opportunity to teach in a non-frontal manner (i.e. not a formal lecture, but an engaging, interactive discussion) I was politely told to keep the method traditional even if the content was to be novel. I'm sure even that has changed by now.

Hebrew

The subject of Hebrew language and literature was a leitmotif that traversed my field experiences. Even though I had informed JDC headquarters that I had a working knowledge of French, Hebrew was my second language when I arrived in Morocco in 1981. Fortunately, my role as pedagogic consultant involved me primarily with the schools, where many of the teachers spoke Hebrew. While the Sephardic pronunciation made clear distinctions between an aleph (א) and an ayin (ע) and between a chet (ח) and a chaf (כ), and while I had a better chance of hearing ancient Mishnaic Hebrew than modern Israeli street slang, I felt at home with teachers and principals who revered the language.

There was great respect for textual Hebrew both in the Moroccan synagogues and schools. Many Moroccan men could easily chant from the Torah with little or no preparation. The Friday evening chanting of the entire eight chapters of Song of Songs in the synagogue gave me a thrill each time I heard it, especially since this was a Biblical work that I had spent many years studying and teaching.

It always amazed me when Israeli guests arrived in a synagogue and the rabbi changed his Shabbat sermon from Arabic or French to Hebrew. I was surprised that the rabbi had such eloquence in spoken Hebrew and overjoyed to see how many congregants understood. Indeed, at times when the local pedagogic practice frustrated me, I reminded myself that the Hebrew outcomes were much better than those we achieved in the West with all of our sophisticated methods.

The profound awe that Moroccan Jews had for the sacred Hebrew word is best illustrated in a local custom that I discovered while preparing for one of our youth encampments at Immouzer. A Torah scroll was required for the Monday, Thursday, and Shabbat services, and one was provided by a synagogue in Fes, a short drive away. In preparation for the transport of the Torah scroll, it was opened and hot wax was dripped on a single letter of the holy text. My surprise at seeing this was nothing compared to the shock of seeing the wax removed later at camp with a sharp instrument. I was sure the letter underneath would go the way of the wax. All of this was to render the Torah scroll unfit for the trip so that a kosher Torah would not be subjected to the indignity of travel. Years later I wondered if something similar could be done to me in preparation for some of my Siberian trips!

This Torah trip reminds me of a mission the JDC gave me during my years in Paris. I received a phone call from the woman at New York headquarters who dealt with the secret operations that had to do with rescuing Jews in distress. She told me that the JDC needed two Torah scrolls that were kosher – that is, fit to be read ritually – for an unnamed distant community, and that the JDC wanted them at no cost. Since an average scroll costs at least thirty thousand dollars, I wasn't sure where or how I would fulfill her request. I put the word out.

Surprisingly, an old Tunisian scroll being repaired for a Paris synagogue was made available as a gift to the Joint, and then a world-famous banker donated a new Torah scroll that he had commissioned in memory of his mother. I was to pick up the latter scroll from the vault of a large bank in Geneva. I spent quite a few hours searching Paris for a hockey kit bag (memories from my Canadian childhood) that I thought would house the scroll nicely on the flight from Geneva.

On arrival at the bank I was taken directly into the vault and was given the scroll. I wrapped it in a prayer shawl, applied no wax (!), and left for the airport. I had completely forgotten the French customs and immigration pre-clearance at the Geneva airport. The customs officer noticed the strange wooden rollers sticking out of my hockey bag and inquired about the contents. I truthfully answered that it was a manuscript. "Rare?" he asked. "Oh, no!" I answered. "You can find many of these in any synagogue." He then asked about its value. I think God Himself put the words in my mouth – "Only spiritual value." "Alors, allez...."

Only much later did I learn that these two Torah scrolls were our entry card to Yemen, an ancient community from which we had been severed for many years by harsh political realities. It is fascinating that in such a community our entry card was not promised millions, but rather the sacred Hebrew word.

When the JDC re-entered Soviet territory in 1988 we already knew that Hebrew instruction had been going on secretly for many years. It was one of the hallmarks of the refuseniks who were trying to leave the Soviet Union for Israel. We also knew that the miraculous revival of the Hebrew language at the turn of the twentieth century and the cultural Zionism that produced and nurtured it was mostly the work of Jews from this part of the Jewish world, Eastern Europe and Russia. It was the anti-Semitism of Communism that had closed down Jewish schools, murdered Jewish authors, and imposed decades of Jewish ignorance on three generations of millions of Jews. What we did not know was the extent of the thirst for Hebrew that existed in every Jewish community that we encountered. I remember a visit to Kharkov, Ukraine in 1989 in which my colleague, Asher Ostrin, and I met with the head of the local Hebrew Teachers Union, an eighteen-year-old who had learned Hebrew two years previously. He took us to a meeting of the teachers that was conducted in Hebrew, with stops for corrections in grammar and diction. When Asher asked one of the young teachers how it could be that his Hebrew, which he had learned only recently, surpassed Asher's own (he had studied for many years), the answer was: "Yes, but you didn't study in Kharkov!" Several months before our visit, about forty people were studying Hebrew. By the time we arrived, five hundred Jews were in classes with another three hundred on waiting lists.

In the 1990s it is entirely possible that more people were studying Hebrew at any given moment than at any other moment in Jewish history. How well I remember sitting in on Hebrew classes taught by locals or Israelis, watching young men and women teaching parents, grandparents, and children all in one room. One class in Novosibirsk in 1990 was especially poignant. The instructor was a trained English teacher who had taught herself Hebrew and was among the first to organize the birth of a Jewish community in this large Siberian city. (How many Jewish communities had the privilege of being organized by Hebrew teachers? The Talmud teaches us that the teachers of Hebrew letters are the true guardians of the city.) In her class one afternoon I heard this dialogue in Russian-accented Hebrew:

STUDENT: In the morning I eat sausage with milk.
TEACHER: Very bad! Jews don't eat sausage with milk.

This, of course, was not religious indoctrination. It was merely the humor of a talented teacher who knew that Hebrew language was more than mere translation of phonemes, but a portal into an entire world of values. Sadly, this point was missed by those in Israel who wrote the first Hebrew textbooks designed specifically for Russians. Hebrew was presented as any other foreign language without reference to Jewish values, Jewish holidays, or even Israeli national holidays. So many of the

Elementary school in Morocco, 1980s.

A Jewish Sunday School class in Cheliabinsk welcomes Seymour Epstein (note my Hebrew name, Shlomo, written on the blackboard), 1992.

texts produced by the JDC education staff in the 1990s attempted to fill that void with non-coercive, pluralist Jewish and Zionist content.

In 1992 I was interviewing candidates for a training program that the JDC, the Melton Program at Hebrew University, and the Jewish Agency had jointly established. We took new Jewish educators from various FSU cities to train them in Jerusalem for two periods of study. I was joined by a Jewish Agency worker and a representative of the University faculty for these interviews, in which each candidate had a fascinating story of Jewish reawakening. One woman from Ukraine told us that she was suddenly shocked to realize that she knew how to say good morning in several ethnic languages of the USSR, but not in her own language. Another teacher from Tashkent was told by her boss after the fall of the Soviet Union that all future work in her plant would be in Uzbekit. That was the day she registered to learn Hebrew in an ulpan. A woman from St. Petersburg told us that the first time she saw Hebrew letters, they spoke to her.

I remember, too, the day an Israeli scholar came to give a lecture in one of our Siberian communities. After the lecture, which had been translated simultaneously into Russian from Hebrew, a grandfather and grandson approached the speaker to tell him, with great pride, that they understood much of his original Hebrew – the grandfather because his youth in pre-war Poland had included Hebrew schooling and the grandson because of a Jewish Agency ulpan he was currently attending. The Hebrew letters had returned home to bind the Jewish family together once again.

My North African experience included some work on the island of Djerba, where the region's oldest community, which goes back to ancient times, still maintains an active Jewish life. Jewish education in Djerba is a fascinating story because it is one of the only places in the Mediterranean basin where the Alliance Israélite Universelle was banned in the nineteenth century by local rabbis who were frightened by Western heresy. Although the ban exists to this day, modern spoken Hebrew came on to the island through a very different portal. A young Djerban named David Kiddushim met a member of the British Army's Palestine Brigade during World War II and was fascinated that this soldier spoke the sacred tongue of the Bible, the Mishna, and the prayer book as an everyday language. Kiddushim found ways to acquire dictionaries, modern Hebrew literature, and textbooks in Hebrew (mostly via a JDC worker of the period) and decided that he would be the one to bring spoken Hebrew to this traditional community, which knew the language only as a sacred text. On my visits I would see him converse at home with his wife in Hebrew. As he walked through the village, Jews who spoke Arabic everywhere else would greet David – the Eliezer Ben-Yehuda of Djerba – in Hebrew.

However, his real contribution was in educating young girls. When he realized early on that he would have more success in his Hebrew revolution with the education of girls, he opened a school in which all instruction was in Hebrew. Even though secular instruction was banned on the island, David felt that arithmetic and geography taught in Hebrew would go unnoticed. Of course, after decades of this new tradition (and as happened in other countries at other times in modern Jewish history), the female Jewish population of this ancient, traditional community is much better trained than the men in both modern Hebrew and general knowledge. Scores of his students became Hebrew teachers both on the island and elsewhere in the Djerban diaspora.

Tatiana, the Sunday school director in Perm in 1993, summed it up. "You learn Hebrew with your heart, not your head. It's difficult, so the head is not enough."

■ ■ ■ ■ ■

There were moments in Morocco in which the urgency of the role of education became all too evident. I once brought all of the senior educators to a meeting with a mission of donors from the United States.

We were eating lunch in the beautiful surroundings of the Ecole Normale Hébraique (ENH) of the Ittihad system (Alliance Israélite Universelle in Morocco) when one of the ENH principals asked to be translated. He rose to say that he and his colleagues were, of course, thankful for the assistance offered by UJA and the JDC. He also wanted us to know that as much as this help was *tzedaka* (charity), it was also an excellent investment in the future of the Jewish people. He spoke of the students as the best raw material in the Jewish world, unspoiled by Western excess, tutored in Jewish classics, and coming from traditional homes of genuine Jewish practice. He realized that after high school graduation they would all leave, some for Israel, others for France, but with the help of the schools they would leave with their bags packed full of Moroccan Jewish culture, ancient texts, and divine values.

On another occasion a school director showed me a building on his campus that the JDC had refused to fund because it was built during the difficult period of the sixties. The policy was not to build infrastructure in a threatened, disintegrating community, but the director pointed out that since its construction, hundreds of students studied in its classes and went on to build Jewish life on other shores.

Although the story of how the culture is faring in Israel, France, Québec, and other places is not the subject of this book, my experiences in French classrooms did not leave me optimistic. In 1988, only eighteen percent of French Jewish children were studying in day schools. Of those, a considerable number were in schools with very few hours of Jewish studies and Hebrew language. The supplementary school system based in Consistoire synagogues was in a shambles and probably counter-productive for both literacy and Jewish identity. Going to public schools in those days meant Saturday attendance, which destroyed the traditional family Shabbat of Moroccan life. In many of the day school classes I observed, the students could not comprehend original Hebrew texts with any ease and most of the teaching was in French around French texts and translations. I noted with particular sadness the absence of any history text illustrating the long and rich years of North African Jewish life. That culture continues to flourish in both the Diaspora and Israel, but much of it is an empty shell of old traditions with little content knowledge to back it up. Add to that the highly assimilative power of French society, the open world we all inhabit, and the current waves of anti-Semitism, and one can imagine a great Jewish culture at risk. Ignorance, assimilation, indifference, and emigration could combine to destroy much of what is left of an important and beautiful element of Jewish civilization. However, there is still a strong base, and revivals of culture have been based on much less. Who knows?

■ ■ ■ ■ ■

As difficult as it was to watch the enrollment figures decrease each year in Morocco and to track the disintegration of that noble community, it was very much the opposite in the first years of our Russian work. Here we were watching the frozen form of a community thaw before our eyes and revive into Jewish forms of life that we could not have imagined. Exhilaration, pride, and astonishment were the emotions most associated with the re-birth of Jewish education in former Soviet territories. They started with schools; we started with books.

In the first few months of our work, in 1989 and 1990, I noted impatience on the part of several communities to put a quick end to the illegal Hebrew classes in private apartments and to open legitimate schools. One might have thought that small communities would sponsor supplementary schools on Sundays and on weekday afternoons, while larger communities would wish to open day schools. However, two small communities, Riga and Tallinn, pioneered the day school movement in the former Soviet Union. Both Latvia and Estonia, which had hosted established Jewish communities before the war and before Soviet domination, realized that a day school was a first step in the right direction.

When I look back at those years, I realize that no one in the Jewish Agency, the JDC, or the Israeli government had to tell these Jews that Jewish education was both essential and strategic to Jewish life. They just knew it in their souls and immediately acted on it.

While we did not see our role as one of establishing schools, we wanted to assist in the realm of Jewish literacy. In the dark period of Soviet repression, we were already involved in the shipping of Russian books on Judaism and Zionism via secret channels. Now, we could build Jewish libraries openly and provide students with the texts that they needed to reconnect to the Jewish people.

At one point, we were shipping thousands of books a month and supplying entire schools with a full complement of Bibles, prayer books, history texts, readers, Hebrew language primers, and holiday guides.

By January of 1992, the Jewish intellectuals of St. Petersburg had organized a scholarly conference on Jewish education. Someone had collected a small library of books related to Jewish schooling for the use of the conference, and on the first day of the conference I noticed a set of Hebrew readers published by the Reform movement in the United States. I liked the series and thought that it would be useful in FSU schools since it blended Hebrew reading skills with authentic and child-relevant Jewish values. It was also colorful and age-specific. I was pleased that someone had discovered the series and that the conference participants would be exposed to yet another good resource.

But by the second day of the conference, the set was missing. There were several possible reasons for this. Someone might have stolen it, one of the many Orthodox teachers might have been offended by the Reform provenance of the books and removed them, or one of the Zionist organizations might have objected to the American source and felt that only Israeli texts belonged at such a conference. While whatever had happened was improper, something about it still appealed to me. Disputes over Jewish texts are the sign of a vibrant community, and even if the perpetrator was an outsider, this kind of exposure to Jewish

First siddur ceremony in the FSU. Tallinn, 1991.

Anatoly Friedman, director of the Riga Jewish School, 1991.

diversity and passionate disagreement was an auspicious beginning for a community of scholars.

■ ■ ■ ■ ■

The school in Riga is mentioned above, and it is worthwhile to describe that early experiment both because of its miraculous uniqueness and because its story is similar to other heroic beginnings during the Jewish revival of the early 1990s. My notes on the Riga school date from January of 1990. The building that housed the pre-war Yiddish school of Riga was given back to the community in 1989 in what was still Soviet Latvia. The school opened with approximately four hundred children, twenty of whom were non-Jews. When I asked what motivated so many parents to opt for a Jewish day school, I received several answers:

- Jewish children will feel more comfortable with other Jewish children.

- Jewish national and ethnic identity is important, and the school will foster it.

- Parents expected a higher level of academic study in a Jewish school.

- There was a desire to change the teaching methods from the Soviet style to more progressive ones.

- They wanted classes of twenty-five pupils per classroom instead of the Latvian norm of thirty-five to forty.

The Soviet Latvian government paid all salaries, including those of the Jewish studies teachers. While the community had to cover certain expenses, it was decided not to charge tuition, but rather to raise the required funds through donations. Indeed, a new joint venture (the term for private business in those days) owned by Jews contributed considerable sums of money to the school in its first years of operation.

Five languages were taught in the school; Latvian, Russian, Yiddish, English, and Hebrew. The first principal appointed had been a teacher in the pre-war school in the same building. His first act was to declare it a secular, Yiddishist school, hold classes on Saturdays, and put up Yiddish signs on every door and wall in the building. He was a very old man who had no contact with Diaspora Jewish education since 1939 and while his ideas were somewhat anachronistic, his passion was limitless. He was enacting a dream he had held on to for five decades. Ultimately, the parents' association ousted him and made the school conform to contemporary models. The JDC arranged a trip to Stockholm and Copenhagen for four new Jewish educators in the crumbling USSR so that two Scandinavian models could be observed.

The Riga school received hundreds of visitors in its first year of operation, 1989–1990, many of whom made grandiose promises of assistance. While very few actually delivered, the community had decided to make this school the cornerstone of its revival. Had they perhaps learned Psalms 118:22 – "The stone that the builders rejected has become the cornerstone"?

As I indicated above, no one taught the Rigan Jews the critical importance of Jewish schooling – they simply knew. Nor did any UJA expert come to teach them how to raise money. The funds flowed into the school as an enthusiastic part of the desire to become Jewish once again. Jews who take their heritage for granted could learn a lesson from this passion.

The JDC has a long history of involvement with early childhood education, most of it inspired and led by Evelyn Peters, of blessed memory, who died soon after I left the organization. Evelyn was one of the great unsung heroes of twentieth-century Jewish life, having worked in the JDC field operations of Iran, Germany, France, North Africa, and India. As one of my early mentors in the organization, she visited Morocco in order to continue her supervision of nurseries and kindergartens there. Although she was self-effacing and modest, her contributions to early childhood education in developing countries were of enormous significance.

It was in one small garderie in Meknes where she showed me her working style, efficiency, and effectiveness. Not satisfied with most of what she observed, Evelyn sat with the school director, the garderie staff, and myself, and gave us her orders for the work to be done over the next year. All of this was accomplished in the most polite fashion with her heavily accented French (although she sounded like a tourist, I knew she enjoyed Molière) and with full respect for everyone involved. She had a way of giving school directors honor while emphasizing the need to give the same respect for garderie instructors, who received hardly any.

Although I knew very little about early childhood education, Evelyn showed me how my pedagogic principles could be applied just as effectively to four-year-olds as to primary-school children. She challenged me to effect real change in the early childhood settings under my supervision in Morocco.

I remember Meknes because when Evelyn and I returned a year later, we found a completely different environment; better furnishings, brighter surroundings (Evelyn hated low-watt bulbs!), cleaner rooms, more order, an enthusiastic and self-confident staff, and happier children. But Evelyn took it a step further. Proud of the progress that had been made in this provincial town, she asked that the next Moroccan early childhood seminar be held in Meknes rather than in Casablanca, as was usual, so that the teachers and their proud community could show off their new garderie.

As an aside, I must say what an experience it was to travel with Evelyn. The long car trips from Casa to various provincial towns, or the short plane hop from Malaga to Melilla, were always filled with stories.

She told me about how she traveled long distances in Iranian deserts with a huge umbrella in the car so that she could pee in privacy where there were no bushes. When she entered a hotel for the first time, she gave her universal requests: a single bed, many blankets, many lamps (she sometimes traveled with high-wattage bulbs of her own.), and toasted baguette in the morning. Once in Meknes, the hotel staff understood that all of Mlle. Peters's guests also wanted toasted baguettes at breakfast and prepared enough bread for all of the teachers at our seminar. It was Shabbat morning and our Moroccan teachers had no intention of eating bread before morning prayers. Evelyn was beside herself with worry about the waste until the kind waiter explained that the hotel staff was very happy to eat her toast with Meknes jam.

In 1990, then, it was natural to start thinking about how the JDC could help Soviet Jews in this sphere. In addition to our history and reputation in early childhood education, there were other factors which encouraged us. The first, mentioned before, was that early childhood settings in the USSR were a well-developed educational sphere that was somewhat free of Marxist-Leninist doctrine. While there were some differences with current thinking in the West, there was a great deal of love for small children and much respect for what could be accomplished in sound educational settings. Another important factor was that the Jews had already begun, on their own, to think about Jewish settings for nurseries and kindergartens. In some communities the authorities had already given permission to establish a Jewish section of a municipal setting, a right given to other ethnic groups as well.

My first visit to a Jewish kindergarten in Vilna revealed to me the potential for working with both the Soviet early childhood traditions and the newly-found Jewish consciousness of a tiny community in revival. I found a setting that operated from 7:00 AM to 7:00 PM, five days a week. My surprise came later that year when I discovered that the two- to six year-olds were being sent to an early childhood summer camp outside the city. Their parents could visit in the evenings on the electric tram that served dacha country. Four teachers, one director, two cooks, two cleaning women, and one part-time nurse – all for thirty-five children, and all paid by the local government, since this was a section of a municipal nursery/kindergarten. The languages taught were Russian, Lithuanian, and bits of Yiddish – no Hebrew yet. Grandmothers (the classic, loving Russian babushkas) came to sing to the children in Yiddish, sharing the songs from pre-war Vilna that they had preserved in memory for this liberated time. Although little boys donned kippot to eat their pork sausage meals, no one noticed the irony.

I was so moved by the experience that I wondered whether we had anything to contribute. The walls were already full of Israeli posters, and the child-size furnishings were better than many I had seen in Canada and France. Nevertheless, I knew that not all cities had the pre-war memories of Vilna, and that even in Vilna, many life cycle and calendar events had been forgotten and needed to be recovered and added to the curricula.

By the summer of 1993, we had a team of early childhood consultants who had prepared much material in Russian and who were leading the first seminar in Zvinigorod, outside of Moscow. Early childhood teachers and directors from fifteen FSU cities were in attendance for several days of intensive training.

My own personal high was an opportunity to teach this group and share with them some of the values, both Jewish and pedagogic, that I see in early childhood education. I also had the chance to pass on one of my traditions and teach this very musical group my favorite nonsense song, "Pikolomini." I have taught that song to youth groups, scouts, teachers, camp counselors, and children around the world, and one of my best moments was being stopped in the streets of Paris by a young man who had learned the song in a Moroccan scout camp. He saw me and immediately called out, "*Bonjour, Monsieur Pikolomini!*"

By teaching those wonderful kindergarten staff that song, I was attempting to link them with an entire history of Jewish instruction, a history they had just joined and apparently intended to creatively alter with their new-found empowerment as Jews.

Here too, in the FSU, our staff made changes. By the second annual seminar, these early childhood settings across many time zones were calling themselves "*ganim*" (Hebrew for kindergartens) and creating curricular materials that were a magical blend of Russian culture, the local climate, the Jewish calendar, and Israeli vistas. There were, of course, some strange quirks here and there.

Many FSU ganim continued to have Christmas trees, since the evergreen in every Soviet home had a more secular significance attached to the mid-winter, New Year vacation than it does in the Christian culture of the West. Many a *Chanukiah* was lit in the shadow of a Christmas tree throughout much of the 1990s.

Another oddity was the naming of the second gan to open in Kiev. Since the first had been established by the local synagogue, the second one decided to call itself The Non-Religious Gan of Kiev. What had transpired was that a visiting secular Israeli educator was working in Kiev at the time. She had noted that the first gan was run by a synagogue and, following the Israeli model, had convinced the locals to call the second gan a secular one. Of course, this appellation had nothing to do with the curricular content of the kindergarten. The children still recited blessings for their food and learned all about Shabbat and the religious festivals. Although the parents in both ganim were equally ignorant of all Jewish knowledge and were all newcomers to Jewish consciousness, the name stuck for a while.

■ ■ ■ ■ ■

I have written elsewhere in this book about the dangers in imposing a cultural context where it does not fit, and the story of the Kiev gan is a prime example. Elsewhere, though, and in more general terms, we found this phenomenon to be an obstacle to the development of Jewish education in new communities.

As self-congratulatory as this may sound, I think that the JDC had the best approach to these issues because of its community-based mandate. Different kinds of schools were being established in the early days of freedom of religion in the FSU. Those that were founded by external organizations, be they Chabad, the Reform movement, ORT, or the Israeli government, had the goals of those bodies as an agenda. Serious problems arose in the schools that were established by locals and that foreign groups attempted to co-opt, adopt, or take over. The original attitude of the Jewish Agency for Israel was that the FSU was strictly a field of operation for aliyah, the assumption being that Jewish schools were not necessary for a population packing its bags. Of course, ulpanim (short-term, intensive Hebrew language classes) were an exception, and many Hebrew language initiatives started by locals with multiple goals soon became the sole property of the Jewish Agency with one single goal: language acquisition for the purpose of settlement in Israel. The stress was on modern, spoken Hebrew alone.

Lishkat ha-Kesher (the Israeli government's Liaison Bureau) had been an important quiet operation during the Soviet years, designed to maintain ties with Jews in various communities. It supported refuseniks, encouraged aliyah, and secretly spread Jewish and Zionist literature with its clandestine collection of books, *Sifriat Aliyah*. After the fall of Communism, it attempted to continue its role in an overt fashion, but spies are not educators. Its members, who knew nothing about Diaspora Jewish education and were too arrogant to ask, took the Israeli schools, and the secular ones at that, as their only model.

In its desire to make transitions simple for Russian children, it named the new schools *batei sefer ma'avar* (transition schools) and *batei sefer mechina* (preparatory schools). One can see how the names themselves de-legitimized the efforts of autonomous communities to define themselves through their schools. However, one cannot be overly harsh in criticism, since the very idea of an independent and voluntary Diaspora community was foreign to the men and women of this government agency.

In contradistinction, we at the JDC were in the very business of community-building. We were in total agreement with both the Jewish Agency and the Lishka (this latter of which we funded generously) that the first priority was emigration to Israel, but from long Joint experience, we knew that many would stay behind. (Actually, one only had to read post-Cyrus sections of the Hebrew Bible to know that fact.) For various reasons, certain Jews either postponed their aliyah or rejected the idea entirely. The aged and the ill were only a part of that percentage. The Joint's mandate was to work with those Jews *in situ*, and the only meaningful way to do that was to help them develop that which has always sustained and nurtured Jewish life – community.

When developing communities established Sunday schools, libraries, synagogues, cultural centers, ganim, and day schools, it was our responsibility to respond by supplying expertise, supplies, books, and program assistance. We saw these developments and the parallel activity in social welfare as the signs of a maturing community and we had much to offer in the way of models from other Diaspora settings. Neither the Jewish Agency nor the Lishka had our mandate and our agenda, which prompted many locals to give us the back-handed compliment of being the least offensive of the foreign intruders!

Just as often as we argued the issues with our colleagues in other organizations, we deliberated internally as well. As the 1990s came to a close, there were greater demands on our resources, many of them the life-and-death situations that arise in social-welfare work. It was neither the first time nor the last that I was asked to measure the outcomes of educational assistance vis-à-vis the obvious needs in feeding the poor and caring for the sick. One can easily determine the effect of extra calories in a diet that has been supplemented by monthly food parcels. It is much more difficult to track the influence of a single book on a Russian-Jewish soul. This is an age-old problem that is encountered and struggled with by anyone who budgets for a community, but in this case the fragility of existence, both material and spiritual, had its own special effect on the severity of budget decisions.

However, two moments serve as a summary to our educational work in the FSU of the 1990 and as evidence of outcomes that justified the great expense of energy and funds. I was attending yet another St. Petersburg Jewish education conference in January, 1996. Listening to the translation of a paper on the teaching of history, I recognized some obvious quotes from a paper of mine on the use of primary sources in teaching Jewish history. I asked the conference coordinator, Ilya Dworkin, about the references and he explained that the young educator giving the paper had heard me speak on the same subject five years previous at the first Dworkin conference. Since then, my paper had been published in Russian in their periodical, *Ivreiski Shkola*, and a group of Petersburg educators had been meeting for several years developing these ideas into curricular reality. That one story is symbolic of the effort and the effect; a measurable outcome if I ever saw one!

In December of 1998, I was in Moscow, once again interviewing a slate of candidates for the Hebrew University Melton Program, young FSU educators destined for training in Jerusalem. We interviewed thirty-four and chose fewer than half. Two of the candidates whom we rejected because of age were eleven in 1990. While they were rejected, Katia and Louba were exceptional stories. While both had passed their formative years under Communism, they had spent their informative years in a Jewish school. One was a student at Adayin Lo ("Not yet" in Hebrew), one of the first Sunday schools established in what was then Leningrad. (The name of the school was taken from a famous quote by Franz Rosenzweig [1886–1929] who, when asked whether or not he put on tefillin (phylacteries) daily, answered, "Not yet." The other young woman was a day school graduate from the same city. They should have been given a prize since they were the first graduates of the new Jewish schools of the FSU, our first encounter with the "product" of the rebirth of

Jewish life. When Katia told me that her Sunday-school experiences were the most important educational exposures of her youth – far more instructive than her many hours in a state school during the day – I knew with great certainty that all of the efforts that hundreds of educators had invested in this historic endeavor were more than worthwhile. They were of critical importance to the entire corpus of the Jewish people in Israel and abroad.

Early on in the FSU adventure, I came to realize that the Russian-speaking Jews in Israel, the new communities in the FSU, and the growing numbers of Russian Jews in other Diaspora countries such as the United States, Germany, and Canada constituted a significant population sector in world Jewry with great potential for developing their own unique voices around the planet. Their influence on Israeli politics is already evident; their presence in the world of Israeli culture and education is felt more each day; their role in changing the face of German Jewry is obvious, and places like Brooklyn and Toronto will soon begin to see new Jewish paths developing. It's entirely possible that as they influenced Zionism and the development of Hebrew at the turn of the last century, Russian Jews will reassert themselves in entirely different ways in the twenty-first century. I like to think, with some pride, that our work in the FSU and that of many others had something to do with that potential.

I am ending this chapter with some selected material that I wrote during my years of service. This first article I wrote at the request of JDC headquarters in the mid-1980s. Written under a pseudonym, it appeared in *Jewish Education Worldwide; Cross-Cultural Perspectives*, edited by H.S. Himmelfarb and S. Dellapergola and published by University Press of America, 1989. At the time, there were some security concerns about using my real name, since I was still serving in Morocco.

The Present State of Jewish Education in Morocco
By Shlomo Philipson[2]

In the mid-1980s there were approximately 2,350 Jewish children in the Jewish schools of Morocco. The transition from the small study rooms (*cheders*) of the past to today's relatively modern schools where both Jewish and general studies are taught is an important chapter in the history of the Moroccan Jewish community. All of the significant events in both the general and Jewish history of Morocco such as French colonial control, mass emigration, the disappearance of rural and village Jews and Moroccan independence had an effect on the schools.

In modern Morocco private schooling is the norm for Jewish children. Most families send their children to Jewish schools, while a significant minority uses the French Cultural Mission schools. There are virtually no Jewish children in the state-run Muslim schools.

There is some government support for the Alliance schools, but the other three systems (Lubavitch, ORT, and Ozar HaTorah) are funded completely by private sources. Any control that the government asserts is implicit and not overt. Obviously, Arabic must be taught and Israel-related topics are avoided.

The official policy of the kingdom is that Jews are citizens with full and equal rights. At one time, the Jews were a major economic, cultural, and social force in Morocco, and many Moroccans of both religions remember that period with warm nostalgia. With the rise of pan-Arab nationalism and under the influence of the Israel-Arab conflict, the foreign policy of the Moroccan government became anti-Zionist while maintaining an internal policy of philo-Semitism. The relationship of the Jews to the government is as healthy as that of any minority to the ruling authority in an absolute monarchy. On a number of occasions, King

---

[2] This article originally appeared in *Jewish Education Worldwide: Cross-Cultural Perspectives*, edited by Harold S. Himmelfarb and Sergio DellaPergola (Lanham, MD: University Press of America, 1989). It is reprinted here with permission.

First Jewish Education Conference in post-Soviet Russia, 1992.

Meknes Teachers' Seminar. Evelyn Peters, Seymour Epstein, Mr. Devico, 1986.

Hassan II has invited all the Moroccan Jews who emigrated to return to Morocco. They would be welcomed by a broad spectrum of Moroccan society, but not by all.

The relationship of ordinary Moroccans to the Jews is much more complex. Since many Moroccans are Berbers, they see themselves as distant from the Arab world (as implied in the Arabic name of the country, Maghreb, which means "West"). They know that as Berbers they share a great heritage with the original Jewish population (pre-fifteenth century). However, others have been more influenced by current trends in the Arab world and do not distinguish between Jews and Zionists. Violent anti-Israel propaganda in all the official media led to justifiable fear within the Jewish community during the 1967 and 1973 Israel-Arab wars.

Even during the 1982 fighting in Lebanon, although the Arab world had virtually abandoned the Palestinians, the Jews were more careful than usual. Although the leaders of the Jewish community speak of Arab-Jewish co-existence, the goal has never been integration. Businesses are run side by side, sometimes even jointly, and among the very affluent, there is some social contact. However, there is almost no intermarriage. One senses great fear and mistrust on the street level. The general uneasiness with the majority culture has been one contributing factor to the almost total enrollment of the community's children in Jewish schools.

It must be remembered that Moroccan Jews were not directly subjected to the two major forces that disrupted the continuity of European Jewry. The enlightenment of Western Europe affected Moroccan Jewry only indirectly through the Alliance schools, and the last major immigration from Europe to Morocco was at the end of the fifteenth century. That immigration from Spain was a source of strength, both in quantity and quality. Unlike many of the Jewish immigrants to America, Spanish Jews saw no reason to leave their tradition behind them. Nor did the Holocaust produce catastrophic consequences for

Moroccan Jewry – even if the community was not entirely spared by the German occupation of North Africa during World War II. Moroccan Jewry remained relatively intact and at peace with its ancient heritage until the mass emigration of the 1950s after the establishment of the State of Israel. Through this emigration, Morocco lost its Jewish population to Israel, France, Canada, Venezuela, and other countries. What remains is a skeleton community that lives on nostalgia, antiquated forms and external assistance.

While all the schools hire Moroccan teachers and teach Moroccan Jewish children, all of them are influenced by foreign sources and funded by Jews abroad. No schools are funded by the local organized Jewish community. A detailed description of each school is given below. The community itself maintains no teacher-training facilities. Although two of the schools run a joint *kollel* for men teachers and the Lubavitch movement has a *michlalah* for women teachers, their effect on teacher training is negligible. The only coordinating body is the Casablanca office of the America Jewish Joint Distribution Committee, which partially funds Ozar HaTorah and Lubavitch locally and directly, and the Alliance Israélite Universelle and ORT globally and indirectly. The local office of the JDC is therefore actively involved in educational work and in coordinating school activities. Each school system, however, maintains its own autonomy and administers its own programs.

Since most of the Jews who wanted to leave Morocco have already done so, a major concern of the community is the maintenance of the status quo. However, even those who have remained realize that their children's future lies elsewhere. Therefore, they want the best Jewish and general education for their children so that the latter will carry on the tradition and be able to make a new life in Israel, France or Canada. Only a very few families opt for the French Mission schools.

THE SCHOOLS

ALLIANCE ISRAÉLITE UNIVERSELLE

The Alliance Israélite Universelle (AIU), which was established in Morocco in 1862, is the only Jewish school which receives government support. The ideological commitment is similar to that of Alliance schools elsewhere, with complementary loyalty to Jewish Moroccan tradition. In 1984 there were four AIU schools in Casablanca, two primary and two secondary. There are also four provincial schools in Fez, Marrakesh, Meknes, and Tangier, where the AIU takes responsibility for secular studies and Ozar HaTorah teaches Jewish subjects. There are small AIU secondary schools in Meknes and Fez. The AIU is responsible for the Jewish studies program at ORT. Including the students shared with Ozar HaTorah (185) and those taught at ORT (224), the total Jewish enrollment at AIU schools in 1983/84 was 1,247.

LUBAVITCH

The Lubavitch movement sent its first emissary to Morocco in 1950. Its present school activities center around a primary and secondary girls' school in Casablanca with 316 students. Lubavitch also runs an American yeshiva with eight students in Casablanca. A *kollel* with approximately forty men is jointly sponsored by Lubavitch and Ozar HaTorah, and a *michlalah* for women has about fifteen students. The girls' schools (Beth Rivka and Seminaire Lubavitch) and the men's yeshiva are the only full-day schools in the Lubavitch system. Though the schools are committed to their own Chasidic master, in Morocco they teach Sephardic customs and rites.

ORT

ORT maintains one vocational school in Casablanca with 224 Jewish students. This school, established in 1947, is administered locally but is under the direction of World ORT in London.

Ozar HaTorah

Ozar HaTorah was established in Morocco in 1947. It is the most Moroccan of all the systems, but is also influenced by its leadership which was trained in France, and its external offices in Paris and New York. There are five schools in Casablanca, two primary and three secondary. The 185 students in Fez, Marrakesh, Meknes, and Tangier are shared with AIU as noted above. Counting these students and eighty more in supplementary settings, the Ozar HaTorah schools taught 1,057 pupils in 1983/84.

All of the systems maintain some dormitories in Casablanca for high-school children from the provinces. The gender breakdown in all of Morocco is about even. There is a constant decline in enrollment as a consequence of rising emigration and a declining birthrate. In 1983/84 enrollment was 12.5 percent lower than in 1982/83.

Informal Jewish Education

There are three active youth organizations in Morocco: the Département Educatif de la Jeunesse Juive (DEJJ), Eclaireurs Israélites (Scouts), and Jeunesse Lubavitch. All three have their headquarters and center in Casablanca, with some minimal activity in the provinces. In recent years, each of the movements has expanded its Casablanca services with the encouragement and financial support of the JDC. Statistics for membership and active participation are not accurate, but it is evident that several hundred children use the three different facilities on a regular basis. The activities during the week, on Shabbat, or on Sundays consist of sports, arts and crafts, communal singing, celebration of Jewish holidays, video screenings, Jewish studies, drama, etc. There are two- to three-week summer camps sponsored by each youth organization as well as others sponsored by a school and a child-welfare society. DEJJ runs a winter leadership seminar, while Lubavitch and the Scouts each run winter camps. There is, obviously, no Zionist youth organization, but youth groups are sent to Israel on an organized basis.

There is very little adult Jewish education. Besides the *kollel* and the *michlalah* described above, two of the local clubs sponsor occasional lectures, but this kind of activity has limited appeal.

PERSONNEL

As in other communities, the lack of qualified personnel is a critical problem for the schools. In Morocco, this issue is further aggravated by continuing emigration and lack of training. Most of the primary schools hire Jewish studies teachers on a full-time basis whereas the secondary schools hire part-time staff for specific areas. The teachers generally have very little secular education, and even their Jewish education is limited to Moroccan yeshivoth, the *kollel* and summer seminars abroad. There is little awareness of pedagogics and no knowledge of complementary disciplines, such as psychology or the media. The one major advantage is that all the teachers are Moroccan and can easily identify with the children and their socio-cultural milieu. The Alliance teachers are usually better trained than the others.

Salaries and fringe benefits are very low by Western standards, but compare favorably with available alternative occupations (unskilled labor). The schools make a sincere effort to adjust salaries to rates of inflation.

The approximate numbers of Jewish studies teachers are as follows:

SCHOOL	FULL-TIME	PART-TIME
Alliance	11	4
Lubavitch	5	4
ORT	1	1
Ozar HaTorah	24	11

Administrators earn considerably higher salaries than teachers, but still much less than their Western counterparts. Their training is generally not much more advanced than that of the teachers under their supervision.

CURRICULAR GOALS AND TEACHING METHODS

Some planning was done many years ago, and the present systems still operate on the basis of decisions made then. ORT sees itself primarily as a vocational school, and Jewish studies has a low priority in their curriculum. The Alliance is devoted to the French system but sees itself as a Jewish school with a serious commitment to Jewish learning. Ozar HaTorah and Lubavitch see their basic *raison d'être* to be Jewish study and practice, but both maintain reasonable standards of general education. Most teaching and learning in Morocco is highly structured, frontal, and based on rote memorization. Attempts to introduce new media, non-frontal models and a basic awareness of child development have met with limited success

SCHOOL CLIMATE

Most Moroccan families are traditional in that they observe Shabbat to some extent and keep a kosher home. Synagogue attendance is also quite frequent. The most observant usually send their children to Lubavitch or Ozar HaTorah, with others using the Alliance and ORT. There are, however, many exceptions. ORT and the Alliance admit Arab students, but there are few overt problems with the mix. The limits of social contact are clear to all parties, and the Arab students feel privileged to study in a quality school. Student interest seems to be directly related to family background. Children from poor homes with illiterate parents are less motivated. The classic problem of understimulation in poor settings has a disastrous effect on certain classrooms. It is important to note that most of the teachers received as limited an education as they are now giving their students.

Despite all their faults, the Jewish schools in Morocco provide general and Jewish instruction of a relatively high caliber to over two thousand children. Most students leave Morocco with the ability to read and understand classical textual Hebrew and even speak modern Hebrew. Their general knowledge is usually sufficient to permit entrance into higher education abroad. In the Jewish sphere, the impact of the school is complemented by active observance of Jewish life in the home and the synagogue. The need for a sound general education is underscored by the fact that emigration continues apace. Moroccan Jewish communities abroad (in Israel, France, Canada, Venezuela, etc.) have suffered a great spiritual loss. The native community is attempting to maintain the grand tradition and to ensure its continuation after emigration.

■ ■ ■ ■ ■

By 1989, posted in Paris, I was working with other senior JDC staff on the beginnings of our re-entry into the Soviet Union, by then under the liberalizing conditions of *perestroika* and *glasnost*. I am including this memo to HQ from the early days of the Soviet operation to expose my early thinking on our educational goals and to illustrate the gap between our first visions and the post-Communist realities which followed.

THE AMERICAN JOINT DISTRIBUTION COMMITTEE
33, Rue de Miromesnil, 75000 Paris – France
November 23, 1989　　　　　　　　　　**CONFIDENTIAL**
MEMORANDUM

To:　　　Michael Schneider, AJJDC – New York
　　　　　Ralph I. Goldman, AJJDC – New York
From:　　Seymour Epstein, AJDC – Paris
Re:　　　Jewish Education in the USSR

Bravo once again to all of us with regard to the November 19th meeting. Just because we can't pronounce any of the names of those cities doesn't mean we won't succeed in our missions!

I promised to quickly write a piece on Jewish education, and here it is. Treat this more as thinking in progress and deliberation rather than as anything final or complete. It is a mixture of what I know as an educator and what I feel as a Jew. I cannot even pretend that it is in any way objective, and because of that, feel the need to elaborate for a moment on my Jewishness.

The Hebrew writers of the earlier parts of this century called themselves the uprooted ones, and the metaphor is suited to most contemporary Jews. I am primarily a spiritual being devoted to God's will and yet totally into this century and Western values. I believe in democracy and pluralism almost as much as in one God. I can easily weep during a Selichot service, but ballet and opera often have a similar effect. While Safed of the sixteenth century holds my spiritual attention, the real Jerusalem of 1989 is where I live (as it were). I love the study of traditional Jewish texts, but my training is scientific, and black-hatted fundamentalism turns me off, both spiritually and intellectually. And yet my love affair with the Jewish people embraces even those who would not tolerate me or consider me authentic (as if they care). You get the idea.

It is precisely because my beliefs are as mixed as the description above that I have very strong feelings about the education of Soviet Jews. (During the heyday of "values clarification" methods, my mentor, Joseph Lukinsky, wanted to start a movement for the obfuscation of values!) Those of us who live in many worlds can best appreciate the need to create educational experiences that integrate realities rather than segregate them, difficult as that may be.

S., whom I respect deeply and admire, has a strong sense of "the last remnant." I cannot speak for him, but I suspect that along with his great affection for *Klal Yisrael*, he believes that intensive Talmudic study must be nurtured whenever and wherever, as a value in its own right. I agree, but cannot place too great an importance on such insignificant numbers while the overwhelming number of Soviet Jews have no knowledge and mostly negative associations with their Jewishness. Education is mostly a business of exposures and connections; some serendipitous, others well-designed! We must maximize the number of friendly encounters that Jews can have with Jewish topics; literature (sacred and secular), history, music, mitzvot, theatre, dance, discussions, etc. Jews then must make autonomous connections to their own lives, to the Soviet system, and to the universe around them. Jewish literacy, like any ability to communicate, produces energy and power in both physical and metaphysical realms. As Jewish consciousness and knowledge increase, the power of Jews to determine their own destinies (read: community building) will grow. (Geometrically, if the job is well done).

So far, anyone can agree, but here I part company. At one point S. said that our aim is to repair the damage that was done by seventy years of Soviet oppression. I disagree only with the choice of metaphor. Repair implies a return to some earlier pristine state. That jibes nicely with Jewish theology that sees the paradise of the messianic era as some form of the earlier Garden of Eden, but it does not work in the world as we know it. First of all, earlier Russia included deathly poverty and disease along with a great deal of Jewish ignorance. It also had its share of Jewish political factions that make today's Knesset battles look like nursery school. All of it adds up to a world that cannot and should not return to us. Soviet Jews, like all students, must begin from where they are and approach modern Jewish life with the tools they presently possess.

Even those tools are changing by the hour. The motivation for Hebrew that existed in the 1960s and 1970s was a thirst unlike anything that ever existed in a Jewish classroom, albeit limited to very few. The paradox of a Rigan learning a beautiful literary Hebrew in two years with tattered texts and no teacher, while a 27-year-old New Yorker who spent an entire career in day schools could not read an Israeli newspaper, is probably a phenomenon of the near past. Once glasnost permits the sale of Hebrew texts in government stores, the guerrilla classes are over. The vacuum is quickly being filled with supplementary schools, adult education lectures, and Jewish Agency teachers. Some of this will work at the beginning, but once the routine sets in there's no reason to believe that such techniques will be any more successful in the USSR than in the USA. Ironically, freedom may dampen motivation and the ability to learn.

One immediate problem is the use of Israeli educators. An observant Israeli teacher may know Jewish sources but has no experience in Diaspora education. A secular Israeli may know how to teach Zionist values in Tel Aviv (not an easy task), but he is not necessarily qualified to teach even secular Zionism in Montreal or Moscow. The different realities explain the sad failure of most shlichim in Diaspora settings. It is not the Zionist message that is problematic; it is the delivery system – not relevant and inauthentic to the lives of the students. While it may be true that JDC cannot influence the selection of teachers because of the split of responsibilities, we should not deceive ourselves into thinking that shlichim are a valid substitution for indigenous teachers.

As certain as I am that Talmudei Torah and eventually day schools will sprout all over the place, they may not be the best model for Jewish education; in contradistinction to Jewish *instruction*. Instruction is what I need in the Russian language. I am highly motivated and need nothing to pique my interest. I don't seek passionate love of the language and I don't aspire to mastery. Education is a completely different game. When America adopted, willy-nilly, the western classroom as its sole model for transmission of Jewish culture, it lost generations of Jewish knowledge and consciousness. It didn't take long for bright kids to figure out that what was taught in public school (or one half of the day in private Jewish schools) was useful, while the subjects taught in Hebrew school were useless. Once the novelty and former motivations in the USSR wear out, the same truth will become apparent to Soviet children. But there is an additional danger in the Soviet system that affects adults as well.

Since 1917 the classroom has been one of the chief agents of indoctrination in the Communist world. The props of rows of desks, a blackboard, and a teacher with chalk in hand represent, for millions of

Soviets, the tools of propaganda. Are we certain that we wish to use the same props for the training of Jewish minds and hearts, young or old? Might it not be the case in the Soviet Union that Jewish education should distance itself from the conventional classroom and search for other loci less identified with totalitarian technique? Even in America it became obvious soon enough that youth groups, summer camps, and community centers were usually more effective in affirming Jewish identity.

Usually we think of informal education as the place to raise consciousness and the classroom as the location for transmission of knowledge, but the overlap has been documented and the distinctions are blurred in the minds of many progressive educators. New creative models that fuse these two realms (only separate because so designated) must be explored. One illustration will help.

To teach the unique phenomenon that Shabbat is for the Jewish people (not only as a commandment to observe for the spiritually motivated, but also as an intricate part of the history of Jewish peoplehood) is almost impossible in a school; *a fortiori*, in a Soviet classroom. While no one credible would do such a thing as declare twenty-five hours out of a week as sacred time, where celebration is just so much state agitprop, and where the blandness of one day's cues routinely follows another, Shabbat is not a phenomenon easily taught by reference to holy texts. Some form of Shabbat will have to be *experienced* for Soviets to taste its pleasures. God only knows what a Shabbaton would be like in Novosibirsk, but creative experimentation is the only way to find out. I chose as my example an educational program that we all know, but the new ones that will have to be created in the midst of Soviet realia are still a mystery.

Some recent experimentation in America is relevant to this illustration. Instead of having children attend Hebrew school classes after school and on Sundays, two or three times a week, a new structure evolved. Children spend some weeks in a Jewish camp-school during the summer, and then over several long weekends throughout the academic year they leave home for four days of intensive Jewish living. This gives them as many hours of instruction and allows for many Jewish experiences (Shabbat, prayer, tzedaka, etc.) that lend utility to the classroom studies. It doesn't interfere with piano and Little League baseball, thereby allowing the child to participate in a variety of worlds. Obviously, the New Jersey model is not suited to Kiev, but an adaptation created in the same pedagogic spirit might be applicable. Only experimentation and time will tell.

The JDC may have a role in the production of materials. But can the materials be produced outside of the learning environment? Should they? Everything that we know about curriculum development warns us to set objectives, establish means, and create materials in constant deliberation with students, subject matter, the broader society, and the teacher. One of the great failures of American general education was the creation in the 1960s of new curricula and learning materials that were not teacher-proof. That is, the teachers took the wonderful new material and sabotaged it by using it with their familiar old techniques. If the WZO sends one kind of teacher and we develop another kind of material distant from the realities of the Soviet Union, we will accomplish nothing. Whatever we do in this particular realm must be carefully coordinated and designed for a master strategy or one of a number of educational strategies for case-specific situations.

Although there is a great deal of work to do, we know that JDC alone will not be able to do it all and that much is already happening without us. Rather than rush us, that fact should slow us down. We have several months of work ahead of us in establishing initial contacts and putting the libraries in place. We can use that time for reflection and careful deliberation so that our educational efforts will be the best we can offer for this momentous opportunity.

Please don't misunderstand my position. I am not opposed to the current proliferation of schools and adult classes. Indeed, I think we should help them with modest materials acquisition when possible. But I see the present JDC-JAFI split of responsibilities in an advantageous light. It gives us the opportunity to reflect carefully on more creative ways to transmit Jewish knowledge and identity.

I would, therefore, like to suggest a two-day meeting the next time we gather for a review. We can spend part of the first day reporting on our library work and analyzing the results. The rest of the time can be devoted to listening to several prominent Jewish educators and some Soviets who would prepare position papers on Soviet Jewish education fantasies for the 1990s and the twenty-first century. The invited educators should be people with expertise and experience in Diaspora Jewish education, and the Soviets should be Israelis who believe in the potential for community renaissance in the USSR. From about 2:30 on the second day, we could sift through what we heard and establish some rough guidelines for a strategy. We could invite some observers from the JA-WZO for the next round of meetings when our deliberations would be more directed.

I implied above that this is not a position paper, but rather some directions of my current thoughts and feelings. To sum up my very tentative arguments:

1. Jewish literacy breeds authentic Jewish power.

2. Soviet Jewish education must be an integrating experience attempting to blend Soviet realia with Jewish values, culture, texts, history, etc.

3. We must operate on many fronts, maximizing the opportunities for Jewish contact rather than servicing only the few who are already actively engaged.

4. There is little need for nostalgia. The Soviet Jewish future will be a unique phenomenon, unlike past models.

5. Glasnost will also have its disadvantages. The "forbidden fruit" aspect of Jewish learning is quickly becoming history.

6. Shlichim are never as good as indigenous teachers. Israelis who are not trained as Diaspora Jewish educators are often counter-productive to Jewish and Zionist objectives.

7. Education is not only instruction, and the classroom may not be the best place for education in the USSR.

8. Formal and informal education are artificial terms that need not act as boundaries.

9. Curricular objectives, educational strategies, and pedagogic materials should be developed in situ with constant reference to students, their society, the subject matter, and the teachers.

10. Our current work allows us the time to reflect on the broader strategies and to develop some special approaches, perhaps more suited to the challenge than the conventional classroom.

11. Developing strategies for millions of dollars of future work does not mean that we cannot currently spend a few well-directed dollars on conventional instruction. Like chicken soup, it can't hurt!

12. Let's invite the brightest to fantasize in front of us. It could be magic!

■ ■ ■ ■ ■

By 1992, Communism had fallen and the facts on the ground had changed. This article from a 1993 issue of *Jewish Education* deals with the first few years of Jewish education in the Former Soviet Union as compared to what I found in the same domain in Morocco.

Jewish Education in Morocco and the Former Soviet Union: Comparative Notes from the Field about Sephardic and Ashkenazic Schooling[3]

PROLOGUE

When I was sent by the Joint Distribution Committee to Casablanca in 1981 as a pedagogic consultant, I could not have dreamt that in 1992 I would be writing an article linking Moroccan Jewish education with what has happened in the former Soviet territory over the past few years. While there seems to be little in common between these two settings, I had the privilege to serve in both of them and have created my own subjective comparisons, contrasts, and connections.

They are, in fact, very different places. Morocco is a small distinct environment which housed no more than four hundred thousand Jews in recent history. The numbers have been radically reduced to approximately seven thousand because of mass emigration since 1948. Those remaining have demonstrated great devotion to their traditions by maintaining Jewish schools, an active synagogue life, and a calendar filled with Jewish celebration. The former Soviet Union (FSU), on the other hand, is a territory spanning eleven time zones that contains no fewer than 1.5 million Jews (or many more if your criteria are the most inclusive). While there has been recent emigration, mostly aliyah, very little connection exists to the various old Jewish traditions of this vast land mass. The reasons are obvious; the current revival of Jewish community life is anything but.

One critical caveat. Fascinated as I am by what has happened to Moroccan Jews in Israel, France, Canada, and Venezuela, I am writing

---

[3] This article originally appeared in *Journal of Jewish Education,* (Philadelphia, PA. www.informaworld.com, 1993). It is reprinted here with permission.

about current Jewish education in Morocco. The same is true of the FSU. The interface of hundreds of thousands of former Soviets and Israel is an ongoing saga of great consequence to the Jewish people, but it is not my topic in this essay.

SUMMER CAMPING

I do not wish to write a definitive description of Jewish education in either locale and will therefore illustrate the flavor of each by comparing them in certain domains. Since Jewish camping is an important part of my background in informal education, I have been actively involved in this activity in both North Africa and in the FSU. The camping tradition in Morocco was that of the French Jewish youth movements (DEJJ and the EIM [scouts]). By the time I arrived in 1981, Chabad had adopted and adapted the tradition to create a strange mélange of French Empire and Messianism in its camp, but the other movement camps operate to this day. In contrast to Jewish camping in the West, the purpose of the DEJJ camp was to integrate and socialize the *Mellah* child into the glories of French culture and manners. For example, speaking Arabic is discouraged in the camps, bizarre as that may sound in a country that has been independent of France since 1956. Great stress is put on quasi-military lining up, marching, bed inspections, ritualistic discipline, etc. These camps, however, are among the most Jewish in the world. Kashrut, Shabbat, and prayer are strictly observed. These elements are not pedagogic instruments as they are in North American camps. That is reserved for the French acculturation. The Jewish elements are as natural as the warm sun and clean air of the Middle Atlas Mountains, where the camps are situated. Because of the traditional nature of this community and its almost unbroken link to the past, Saturday is much more Shabbat than it is Samedi.

My work in the Soviet Union began in late 1989. There are dozens of Jewish population centers that were shattered by every force that ever worked against us; pogroms, emigration, hunger, anti-Jewish legislation,

Nazi genocide, killing writers, arresting teachers, even self-hate. While we can talk of the past glories of Jewish life in some of these places and even about the contributions of Russian Jews to Zionism and modern Hebrew literature, there is almost nothing left *sur place* that links what was with what is.

When I, my JDC colleagues, Jewish Agency shlichim, and Israeli government representatives began to suggest summer camps in 1989–1990, the local Jewish activists seemed wary. Their model of camps was the *Pionersky Lager* of Soviet youth groups. The spartan conditions, constant indoctrination, and ever-present anti-Semitism made the very concept of summer camping anathema to Jewish parents and their children. There were a few experimental camps in the summer of 1990, notably a family boat trip on the Ob River in Siberia and a children's encampment in Estonia. The latter was illustrative of much that has happened in the FSU these past few years.

Tallinn is a small community of about three thousand Jews. It was one of the first to dream of a Jewish day school. Adult Hebrew classes were prevalent by 1989 and some supplementary Jewish classes were being offered to children. One of the Hebrew instructors was a Christian from Finland who had lived in Israel and came to Tallinn to offer her services as a teacher. The community had decided to open the day school in September 1990 and planned a camp during the preceding summer. A Canadian rabbi and some Yeshiva University students came to help with the camp. In contradistinction to the Moroccan experience described above, there was no model of camping to follow. In fact, the camp had to militate against Soviet camping traditions. Parents had to be assured that this was going to be safe fun. The rabbi, to his credit, did not let food become an issue. The children ate what was available, while he and his staff managed on some canned provisions they had with them. He decided to return the sacred time that had been stolen from these Jewish children. Each day became a Jewish holiday that had never been heard of, much less celebrated. Each evening after Rosh ha-Shanah, Simchat

Torah, Purim, and Pesach, the children would call home to wish their parents a *hag sameach*. On the day dedicated to Tisha be-Av, the children visited a nearby Nazi killing site where the Soviets had "forgotten" to mention who was murdered. The children came with Jewish symbols to plant in the ground and instantly turned the place into a Jewish monument.

When the camp ended, the children presented their two weeks of Jewish celebration to their parents in a program of song and dance. The school was scheduled to open with sixty pupils, but the enthusiasm from the camp pushed the enrollment over two hundred. It was as if the entire community had been suddenly transformed. The initiatives were mostly local, but the external assistance was critical to the success.

Since then, there have been winter and summer camps across the breadth of the FSU. There were approximately thirty-five camps in the summer of 1991 and about fifty planned for 1992. They are organized and run by local communities (e.g. Ekaterinburg in the Urals or Novosibirsk in Siberia), the Jewish Agency, Bnei Akiva, Yeshiva University students, the Israeli Masorti Movement, Chabad, etc. The JDC was privileged to provide books and learning materials to almost all of them.

JEWISH SCHOOLS

There has been Jewish schooling of one form or another in both Morocco and the territory of the FSU for at least one thousand years. In both regions, the pre-enlightenment *talmudei torah* or *chadarim* began to change in the latter half of the last century. The major difference, of course, is the lapse of seventy years of Communist rule in the Soviet Union which virtually obliterated formal schooling for Soviet Jewish children.

Morocco still boasts four school systems: Alliance Israélite Universelle, Ozar HaTorah, Lubavitch, and ORT. All of them originated outside of Morocco in order to replace the traditional *cheder*, the last instance of which disappeared from Marrakech during my tenure in the country. As with summer camping, comprehensive detail can be found in other articles and books; I will compare seeming opposites to offer an illustration of the environment.

One would probably line up Ozar HaTorah and Lubavitch on one side with the Alliance and ORT on the other side. The former are seen as religious schools while the latter, still traditional by western standards, are best described as modern settings. The distinction is blurred by the fact that Lubavitch uses the latest techniques and equipment, the Alliance sees itself as a religious institution, Ozar HaTorah's facilities are up-to-date, and ORT's technology is more suited to the Third World than to France or Israel (target countries for graduates). The general perception, however, is that the schools can be divided as I did above.

The Alliance came to Morocco in 1860, in advance of the French Protectorate. It was to do for the Jews what France wished to do for all of its colonies. It came to teach the language and culture of France while permitting the Jews to continue their ancient Berber and Sephardic traditions. For many years, the *cheder* co-existed with the AIU school. In recent times, the AIU has taken a more pro-active position on Jewish Studies and Hebrew language, even seeing itself as the representative of authentic Moroccan Jewish heritage. It's a strange twist, but one that has appealed to Moroccan Jews for the past 130 years. Moroccans saw the Alliance as a step out of the *Mellah* into the French world. The AIU's return to Jewish culture only served to verify that one could live in both worlds at the same time.

Interestingly enough, little attempt has been made to "modernize" the Jewish curriculum. With few exceptions, the style and content of Jewish studies in AIU schools is quite similar to that of the other settings. The teachers are traditional Moroccan Jews, and that fact, more than any ideology or training, colors the course of studies. I remember an incident in which one of the senior AIU educators was attempting to write a doctorate on Jewish mysticism at a French university. He had taken the required courses during summers by correspondence and he had read the primary literature. He was shocked when his professor asked about Platonic influences on the Kabbalah – not quite sure who the Greek was nor what he had to do with the Zohar!

In 1991–1992 there were approximately one hundred Jewish schools operating in the FSU. About fifteen of those were day schools, the rest being supplementary settings of one style or another. Different regions showed different modes and paces of development, but the general direction was from adult Hebrew classes in rented quarters to a Jewish Sunday school for both children and adults (many of them now in permanent facilities). None of this occurred in a vacuum, and it is important to note the internal and external influences.

Contrary to popular opinion, the fact is that most of the initiative, drive, energy, and funding for Jewish schools came from the local Jewish population. At the very time that the organized Jewish world was justifiably encouraging aliyah; when hundreds of thousands of Jews were, in fact, leaving for Israel and elsewhere; when those concerned with the Jews who were staying behind (myself included) could only talk of weak communal structures and lack of western organizational know-how – during that very same period, dozens of communities were organizing and funding their own modest beginnings of Jewish schooling. People who never saw a Jewish textbook, who weren't quite sure if Purim preceded Pesach on the calendar, and who wouldn't know a UJA pledge card if they saw one were building institutions of Jewish learning – not merely schools for Jews, but authentic Jewish schools.

They had some wondrous historical accidents on their side. *Glasnost* and *Perestroika* had declared it permissible to either emigrate as a Jew or stay as a Jew. Like all new license, it became the very thing to do, with a vengeance. Latvians wanted to prove to Moscow that they could take better care of their Jews. Everyone assumed that treating Jews well could lead to better relations with Washington, the Jewish capital for people reared on the "Protocols" rather than Isaiah. This wonderful serendipity of assistance notwithstanding, it is to the credit of hundreds of individual Jews that they seized the moment and started to build.

The schools are dependent on foreign teachers, mostly shlichim from Israel. These are supplied by the Jewish Agency, the Israeli government, and other interested organizations. While every effort is being made to train local teachers by means of in-service training in the FSU and in Israel, the problem of foreign teachers will continue to plague the FSU schools for many years. This is in stark contrast to the situation in Morocco, where except for a few Chabad imports (who have been living in Morocco for decades), all of the Jewish studies teachers are locals. The inability of a foreign teacher to communicate properly, the lack of a common cultural base, and the instability of short-term placements are serious threats to the viability of FSU schools. On the other hand, the case of the Moroccan teacher in speaking to and with his students is a rarity in most Diaspora settings.

LEARNING ENVIRONMENT

In Jewish education one can speak of a dialectic between the values of the school and those of the home and street. In most Diaspora schools the gap between the two settings is great and the dialectic borders on warfare. In certain liberal institutions, some community schools, and most Chasidic schools the gap barely exists; the values and the educational aspirations of both sides are identical. Strangely, in both Morocco and the FSU this rare pedagogic environment is the norm. The exceptions are Chabad and some other fundamentalist settings which demand more of their pupils than the parents aspire to, but in most schools in these two disparate places, the family believes in what the school is doing and supports its efforts. The major difference is that the Moroccan family provides a kosher home, synagogue attendance, and Shabbat observance, while the average Russian home provides Jewish illiteracy, mixed marriages, an uncircumcised father, and the decision to not make aliyah. These latter conditions apply to most families who *do* send their children to a Jewish school. The still vast majority that does not participate in community life can probably add a negative stigmatized attitude to Judaism to the sad list noted above.

How different the Russian culture from Moroccan culture and society! Curiosity, a sense of history, and reading seem to be national traits. We know enough about Russian history to know that the serfs were not readers and that French language and culture had their roles in Russia as well. Nevertheless, the current situation is that most of the Jews and large sectors of the general population are avid learners and natural readers. I have met Russians whose hobby is learning new languages – a new one every two years, never traveling to the country of that language. It makes for strange accents and diction, but it illustrates my point. Russians are fascinated by history, their own and that of other nations. History teaching was abused by the Soviet Communists, and there is a current attempt at correction. The most popular topic in Jewish studies after Hebrew is history. General history teachers, mostly non-Jews, are being re-trained by the Jewish schools to teach Jewish history. While I don't think I knew one teacher in Morocco who had ever read a history text, I have already participated in an advanced seminar on Jewish history pedagogics with ex-Soviet teachers. When you give them a text at a conference, they confront you the next day with erudite comments and notes that show profound understanding of the period and yet deeper ignorance of all the Jewish references! How does one relate the Great Patriotic War to the *Shoah*? The rhetoric and propaganda notwithstanding, the Russian people suffered greatly and mourned deeply, but the Jews were never taught the Holocaust as we have taught it to our children these past forty years.

CONCLUSION

The clearly opposite situations described above with regard to curiosity, history and reading are, of course, linked to modernity. There is much about Morocco that is pre-modern, the Soviet Union was locked into a mid-twentieth-century modernity, and the so-called First World now sees itself as a blasé post-modern civilization. Each has its attractions and liabilities. The post-modern Jew is confronted jointly with the disappearing splendor of the Moroccan Jewish heritage on one continent and the profound quest of the Russian Jew to regain his inheritance on another.

CHAPTER THREE

FIFTY PERCENT

At a certain point in the history of JDC relations with the French Jewish community there was a joke circulating in Paris. It seems that a penniless Jew landed in New York and he was concerned that he would not be able to celebrate Passover properly because of his poverty. He decided to write a letter to God asking for help. "Dear God, please send me one hundred dollars to celebrate Pesach as required by Your law." He addressed it to God and dropped it in the nearest mailbox. By wondrous luck it fell into the hands of a Jewish postal employee who sent it to the JDC headquarters. The workers at JDC were not sure what to do with it, but the director instructed them to send the fellow fifty dollars. After receiving the money and using it to celebrate a fine Passover, our friend decided to write a letter of thanks. "Dear God, thank You very much for the money You sent. It was used well over the holiday. Only, next time please don't send funds via the Joint, since they always deduct fifty percent."

While this joke betrayed the fact that the French did not know that the JDC does not operate programs in the United States and that this branch of American Jewish charity is designated solely for other countries, they did have one fact close enough to the truth. The JDC usually budgeted for percentages of a local project, not for total funding. In disintegrating communities it was felt important for the locals to participate, even if in token amounts or in rapidly diminishing percentages. This was done to maintain local dignity, to preserve and encourage local leadership, and to reduce the drain on JDC budgets worldwide. In new communities such as the FSU, the process may have begun with in-kind participation such as volunteers, office space, or equipment, but the principle remained the same. In those communities it was hoped that the JDC percentage would decrease as the community gained strength, status, and autonomy.

In October of 1990 I had a unique encounter with this principle on a piece of Spanish soil on the coast of North Africa. Melilla is an ancient Moroccan community where approximately one thousand Jews live on a few square miles of Spanish territory on the African coast. One might say that it is Morocco's Gibraltar. The president of the community and I were reviewing the community's annual budget, JDC's contribution, and the cash flow. After noting that fifty percent of the JDC subvention had just arrived by bank transfer, the president told me to instruct New York to send no more money that year. I had just finished describing our latest venture into the Soviet Union and the fascinating work we were beginning. The president informed me that business had been good that year for the local Jewish merchants and that he wanted the money to be used in the Soviet program. That was a JDC moment I will not forget!

In fact, there was great fascination by the Moroccans in our early Soviet work. It could easily have been another planet, but when I took the chief rabbis of Moscow and Leningrad to Strasbourg for a visit, the local rabbi of the Moroccan community in Strasbourg was so overwhelmed with joy about the rebirth of Jewish life in Russia that he gave them a Torah scroll worth many thousands of dollars. This too could have been a fifty-percent story, since it was one scroll for two different communities.

One of the Chabad rabbis in Casablanca bettered my French joke with one of his own. At Purim time he asked me where there is a reference to the Joint in Megillat Esther, the Purim story as recounted in the Hebrew Bible. I was perplexed until he answered that King Achashverosh was always offering Queen Esther up to half of his kingdom – fifty percent!

CHAPTER FOUR

CAMPING IN MOROCCO

I AM INCLUDING this memo to JDC Headquarters on camping in Morocco since it illustrates some of the painful issues in a disintegrating community.

AMERICAN JOINT DISTRIBUTION COMMITTEE

3 Rue Rouget de L'Isle, Casablanca, Morocco

August 24, 1986   <u>**CONFIDENTIAL!**</u>

MEMORANDUM

To: Ralph I. Goldman, AJJDC – New York

From: Seymour Epstein, AJDC – Morocco

Re: Some Reflections on Jewish Camping in the Moslem
            Countryside

I'm writing this sitting on a park bench in Ifrane, where just a few weeks ago Prime Minister Peres met with His Majesty Hassan II. It's hard to describe this immaculate, well-trimmed resort town near the foothills of the Rif range. In a wet winter this town is white and filled with skiers. In the summer the Moroccans come for the clear mountain air and the evening chill. It's not like any other village in the country, but one quickly learns that gross generalizations are difficult to apply in North Africa. This is the land of the specific, the particular, and the here and now. Rules exist, but the exceptions abound.

Ifrane is twenty kilometers from Immouzer, the village of summer camps, where JDC sponsors the Aide Scolaire Colonie de Vacances where some two hundred and fifty Jewish children enjoyed the summer programs of the Ozar HaTorah, Aide Scolaire, and DEJJ camps. (Approximately another two hundred and fifty children were campers in other settings run by Lubavitch, the Scouts, and the Casablanca day camps.)

This past week in Casablanca I met with the leadership of Aide Scolaire to discuss their program for 1986–1987 and to talk about the camp. After reviewing all the details that are important to a good camp program, we got to the heart of the matter. It disturbs them that the Jewish camp is a very modest setting compared to the other camps in the region. They are concerned that our camp staff is not comparable to the very talented people at the neighboring colonies. Why don't our children march through Immouzer in camp uniforms like the children of the Bank of Morocco camp or the Ministry of the Interior camp? Shouldn't we build a new dormitory and a stainless steel kitchen like the sugar industry camp next door? Of all the millions of hungry and unschooled children in Morocco (our average age now is seventeen!) a few thousand of the elite get to spend a two- to three-week period in Immouzer. Among them are some Jewish children, mostly from the welfare files of the Casablanca C.I.

And then the discussion began. I am trying to tell these men that I have a profound respect and love for the Moroccan Jewish past but that my present concerns are for the coming few years. I want to help the existing population to live with the grace that befits such a community but I also want to encourage the young people to prepare for their real future outside and far away from this world. The very children that we see at Immouzer are the ones most in danger. The wealthy spend their summers in Spain and the upper middle class see Immouzer as a place for poor children to learn French manners. These men remember a time when the elite class in this country was the French population and the Jews. The Moroccans didn't run fancy summer camps. From this perspective Immouzer is the ultimate symbol of disintegration and despair; their world turned upside down. Could the JDC help them restore their pride? Yes and no, I answered. We'll do what we can with their help to keep the camp comfortable and safe for the next few years of camping, but we're not investing in major construction in a Moslem country. But what about *our* Peres and *our* monarch? They answered the question themselves before I even reached for the cold water faucet.

On Friday morning, August 22, I traveled to Immouzer for my third visit this season (one for each session) to see how the DEJJ camp was going, to plan for future repairs and renovations, to check on Julie Siegmund, our Jewish Service Corps summer volunteer, and to enjoy Shabbat and Sunday with the children of DEJJ.

One thing that hits you right away is the comparative freedom that these children have here at Immouzer. Within the compound of the camp they can run and skip, play ball, sing Hebrew songs, pray and eat outdoors, and forget about the streets of Casablanca where most such activities are severely restricted. And yet the men of Aide Scolaire (who own the camp) list as their first priority a high security wall around the camp. The Lubavitch camp had a police guard offered as a courtesy by the Pasha of Tangiers. There are no more than ten thousand Jews in a country of twenty-five million Moslems. With me I brought an article from the local Arab press published just last week. I asked Mr. Dayan to write me a French resume, but I already know the article is one of many that spells trouble. The lead photo on page one of the paper was a picture of the three Lubavitch rabbis with the chief rabbis of Morocco and

Casablanca blessing a saint's tomb. It was captioned "Zionist Activity in Morocco from 1926 to 1948." The picture was "borrowed" from the community publicity brochure and was taken in the last five years.

Mr. Dayan has maintained excellent relations with the other camp directors in the region. I accepted his invitation to accompany him on a visit to the camp for children of the employees of the Bank of Morocco, Shabbat morning after services. Mr. Dayan is well known at this camp and the welcome was very warm. We met the director, a resident artist, the director of social services at the bank, and other assorted guests and staff. The facilities are of a high standard. The walls are covered with art and there is a display of camper crafts. The staff is very proud of the camp and its achievements over the years. There is, of course, the rigid discipline and wall charts of statistics that one finds in any French-style camp, but the warmth and human touch are overwhelming. Dayan has told me that on other visits to similar camps the children usually sing at least one song about solidarity with the Palestinian freedom fighters, so I keep looking for a flag or map of Palestine. Not this time. The children file into the dining room in uniform and sit together (boys and girls). They sing songs of welcome in Arabic; the books in the library are primarily in French. Then they beg Allah to bless our arrival and position their hands in something between an Arab praying position and a Protestant grace and thank Allah for their food. They look healthy and confident. The young woman leading the singing and setting the general tone is a professional camp person that I would have sought out in my old Ramah days. After the tour of orderly dorms, a sparkling kitchen (with pastry chef), and the customary sweet tea one of the senior personnel from the bank told me that Immouzer is the place to invest and that the bank is buying adjacent property and expanding the facility.

From the minute I entered that camp I understood my Aide Scolaire friends. When the past is your primary point of reference and the present leads to despair, the future can only be illusion and fantasy. Our Jews who once lived here as cultural aristocrats are now paupers compared to the very people who were once their inferiors. The country is no longer theirs. They cannot invest in Immouzer or in a community centre in Casablanca because their future is elsewhere. As much as they may know this fact, it pains them greatly (me too) to deal with the truth of their own loss of homeland. The future belongs to the children of the Bank of Morocco and not the children of Aide Scolaire.

There are moments when I would like to think that we are overreacting; that the Jews have a future here as a respected minority. Clearly that is the intent of the king. But Moslem fundamentalism and Arab nationalism will probably have their way. The local media and the curses of the street will probably determine the future of the community more than the will of the monarch.

Jewish scouts of Morocco at Immouzer summer camp, 1980s.

Jewish scouts of Morocco at Immouzer summer camp, 1980s.

CHAPTER FIVE

SUKKOT IN THE MOROCCAN PROVINCES

THIS IS ANOTHER MEMO to JDC Headquarters which illustrates life in the provincial communities in the 1980s.

AMERICAN JOINT DISTRIBUTION COMMITTEE

3 Rue Rouget de L'Isle, Casablanca, Morocco

October 30, 1987   **CONFIDENTIAL!**

MEMORANDUM

To: Ralph I. Goldman, AJJDC New York

From: Seymour Epstein, AJDC Morocco

Re: Sukkot in the Provinces

Since I had not been to some of the provincial towns for relaxed conversations in some time, I decided to spend the first days of Sukkot in Tanger and Hol ha-Moed in Tetouan, Fes, and Meknes. Cheryl and Laura Meislin came with me on the trip.

Tanger has less than four hundred Jews left. Needless to say, this is a small portion of what once was. The "nostalgia-illusion" syndrome that I have described elsewhere exists in its most potent form in this community. The Tangerois are all Spanish exiles who live in a city that was once international and very Jewish. From the beach you can easily see the opposite shores of Southern Spain which represent both western Europe and the rich past of these Jews. Many Spanish-zone Jews don't even identify with other Moroccan Jews of Berber origin and refer to them as *Forasteros* (strangers). Tanger is a very dirty port town, and yet the Jews speak only of its glorious past and its eventual revival.

The paradox of a disintegrating community that supports a home for the aged, a small hospital, a welfare program, several synagogues, and a Jewish social club is evidence of the great pride that still exists. The celebration of Sukkot was grander than one could find in any American community ten times the size of Tanger. The community is proud of its central synagogue, Shaar Raphael, administered by Rabbi Yaakov Tordjman, who was trained in a JDC-sponsored program in Casablanca. The sukkah in Shaar Raphael and those of the older synagogues were decorated with beautiful cloths and the traditional Moroccan ornamentation. We ate in four different sukkot and celebrated every moment of the festival with many members of the community. Most of our time, however, was with Mr. Abraham Azancot, the very capable president of the Tanger Jewish community. A quick profile will give you a sense of how fascinating the discussions were. Mr. Azancot is a chartered accountant who teaches accounting and property management. He speaks fluent Spanish, French, and Hebrew. Although he completed his rabbinic studies, he does not use his rabbinic degree. He is a student of the Kabbalah and Spanish Jewish history. Every Shabbat morning he teaches a two-hour class in his home on the *Mishneh Torah* of Maimonides. The class is taught in Spanish except when I am in town. Then he switches to French for my benefit. It was in Tanger that we spoke about community assets. I reported on that in a separate memo.

I had not been to Tetouan for several years. Last year there were three stabbings of Jews in Tetouan, two of them fatal. I was advised against visiting for several reasons. Tetouan is in the Rif region which has its share of smugglers, drugs, political opponents, members of the Moslem Brotherhood, etc. His Majesty has not visited for many years, but is planning a trip in March, 1988. We ate in the community sukkah with three of the only leaders left. There were once eleven thousand Jews in this city. It now counts under two hundred with the majority aged, *hilouk,* or *nistarim.* Most of the Jews now live in Venezuela. The three men gave us varied accounts of the murders and it was up to me to read the fear in their faces. They showed us one of the most beautiful synagogues in Morocco and the huge "casino" (Jewish social club) which was the centre of all Jewish activity a few years ago and is now a relic. They spoke of Spanish Jewish pride and how, when Spanish colonists started to arrive in Morocco in the eighteenth century, they were shocked to find a community that spoke a beautiful dialect right out of the royal court of fifteenth-century Spain. And then they described their most pressing welfare case and their inability to cope with the expenses and the required care.

There's a Jewish orphan who attacked his uncle and is now in an institution for the criminally insane. The last two Jews in that hospital died under suspicious circumstances. Could I help to release him and find another setting for him? As impossible as it sounds, we may have a solution.

Two quotes kept running through my mind as we ate in that sukkah with these heroic last leaders of Tetouan. In a book about Austria, Marie Von Ebner-Eschenbach wrote, "Not fatal, but incurable, these are the worst diseases." "In a place where there are no men, try to be a man," says *Pirke Avot.*

On the way to Fes, we stopped in Volubilis to see the Roman ruins. They are truly magnificent and I mention them here for a purpose. We were shocked by the state of the site. There was a healthy entrance fee and then nothing in the way of explanation. There were no guides and the rusted equipment of the first French discovery team was still strewn around. Not one member of my local staff has ever been to Volubilis. Some have never heard of it. No Jewish school sends trips to visit and no teacher or school principal that I know could tell you what it is. This is a country where the education system discourages curiosity and where history is almost completely neglected. Not only is Roman history forgotten; Jewish children learn very little about Moroccan Jewish history or even about the Moslem conquest. The distant past is meaningless, the near past is cloaked in nostalgia, and the present is depressing. As I have stated before, this makes for an easy transition to a future of illusion.

The visit to Fes consisted mainly of lunch with Mr. and Mrs. Elie Bettan in their sukkah. Fes has a very weak president, Mr. J.B. Fortunately, the JDC's subsidy goes to the Societe de Bienfaisance and not to the C.I. The president of the Societe, Mr. Elie Bettan, is a very active leader with the genuine interest of the community at heart. He is a reasonable man with fewer illusions than most and considering his modest means, a very generous soul. I was happy to be able to give him the good news about the high school scholarship fund and confident that he can be trusted to administer the fund properly.

We discussed the Talmud Torah building and he told me of the community plan to renovate it and create a small community centre for the remaining three hundred and fifty Jews. It sounds good, but with that C.I. and its present leadership it will be a slow process. Given the efficiency of our work in Fes, I sometimes wish that we had a similar communal structure in Casablanca. I have even suggested to the Casablanca C.I. that the Home should be run by a separate committee of C.I., OSE, and JDC members, but to no avail.

The one negative moment in Fes was caused by an unfortunate street scene directed against myself, Cheryl, and Laura. It almost became violent with the threat of rock throwing and the police had to intervene. It was very disturbing, but what I have come to expect from that city; not as unpleasant as Tetouan, but uncomfortable at times. When we think of worst-case scenarios, we usually concentrate our plans on Casablanca, but I hate to think what will happen in places like Fes if and when the bad times come.

The contrast between Mr. Bettan's modest sukkah and the magnificent sukkah chez Mr. Devico in Meknes was astounding. The Meknes president is the head of a large family business that cans jams, jellies, olives, capers, pickles, etc. Mr. Devico presides over the largest and strongest provincial community numbering approximately five hundred souls. There are still two schools in Meknes; a primary school in the new city and a junior high in the mellah. There are several active synagogues, a sheltered housing project, and an air of relative stability in this large industrial city an hour from Fes. The two communities are very different. In fact, Mr. Devico was born a Fassi and is probably somewhat suspect among the born and bred Meknessi. Sound familiar? To this day in Paris some of the internal politics at the FSJU can be traced to differences between the Meknessi and the Fassi.

Much of the discussion at dinner in the opulence of the Devico sukkah was about the president's attempt to put some order into a community board that is divided and even somewhat corrupt. Although there is some grumbling, it seems that most members of the Meknes community support Devico's effort. I have helped them to re-organize the DEJJ and the committee in charge is quite dynamic. The two school directors are also effective even though the teaching staff is very weak in some areas. Evelyn and I have invested much time and energy into the kindergarten and the results are very satisfying.

To balance the material wealth of the dinner, I spent the next morning at 6:00 A.M. Hoshana Rabbah prayers with the more modest members of the community. I beat my aravot on the ground with the best of them and rushed back to Casablanca for a few hours of work and two more days of celebration in my normal surroundings.

CHAPTER SIX

CULTURE CLASH

AS AN UNDERGRADUATE at Columbia University, I had the privilege of studying with Margaret Mead, the anthropologist. Commenting on an incident in which an American Peace Corps volunteer had, in her letters home, revealed genuine shock at the conditions in a Third World country, Mead made the claim that this was not an example of culture shock, but rather life shock. Her point was that a suburban child of America would rarely see food growing, an open wound, the birth of a baby, or a dead body.

My exposure to some of the mild differences between Paris and Toronto, the more exotic cultural gaps in Morocco, and the tragic effects of the Soviet years produced a mixture of culture shock, life trauma, and Canadian Jewish incredulity.

Let's start with my first dead body. My Casablanca barber, a member of the Jewish community, felt quite close to me since I had enabled him to study in a course for ritual slaughterers. I liked to remind him that he killed cows on Wednesday, but this was Friday and all I needed was a haircut. One morning, my office staff informed me that his father had just died. They insisted that I attend the funeral that afternoon, but I had a very important meeting with the U.S. Consul General that could not be postponed. In that case, I was told I had to visit the house of the deceased in order to pay my respects before the funeral (not the usual practice of Ashkenazim), which I did. As I entered I found a distraught group of family members in the living room, but I was quickly taken to the dining room where, much to my dismay, I found the body of my barber's father on the table, half naked. Half, because he was being placed in a shroud as I entered. This part of Jewish mourning and burial practice is not a home activity where I grew up. I backed up, but both the family and my driver (and erstwhile cultural interpreter) urged me forward to get closer. It became apparent that, as an honoured guest (JDC country director), I was expected to participate in this exercise. I was given a large needle with string in it and told to stitch the shroud closed.

This is the time to explain that at a Moroccan bar mitzvah (never on Saturdays), the male guests assist the young boy in putting on tefillin his first time by each wrapping one ring of leather around his arm. Depending on the number of guests, the bar mitzvah must accommodate all of them by removing his arm tefillin several times so that each male guest gets his own turn of the leather. I had performed that relatively simple task many times, and suddenly realized that this was my turn at shroud-stitching.

I managed, even though the poor man's arm kept slipping out. I got someone else to bend the stiffened arm back in, since that was asking too much of my squeamish sensibilities. My driver whisked me out and took me directly to the Consul General. One can guess his hearty greeting: "Good God, Epi, you look like you've seen a ghost!"

Reading and writing turned out to be a cultural bridge for me in my encounter with Morocco and the FSU. Morocco is an oral-aural environment. The main language, Moroccan Arabic, is a spoken dialect with no alphabet or written form. In the last few decades, Moroccans have learned to read and write standard Arabic, but only a short while ago, the common person in the street or in the countryside had no access to reading or writing. To this day, most Moroccans have few books at work or at home. Of course, male Jews learned Hebrew with its alphabet and used it for prayer and study, but even in the synagogue many men prayed long hours by heart and only used prayer books for rare hymns used on special occasions. The upside of this kind of language culture is prodigious memory. I was always amazed by the people's ability to recite full texts that they had learned only once. I was somewhat perturbed that teachers would show up at in-service training seminars without writing implements until one teacher challenged me to ask him to repeat everything I had said.

Strangely, this aspect of Moroccan culture resonated with me personally. I was not a natural reader. I did not grow up in a house filled with books, nor did I read into the night, flashlight in hand. In fact, I always found the reading required for my four university degrees a burden and faked my way through some of it. On the one hand, I could identify with an oral/aural lifestyle, and yet it was in Morocco at the age of thirty-five that I became a reader. It might have been a reaction to the prevailing lack of reading, but more than likely it was a product of my loneliness in a strange country. I had neither phone nor television at home, and reading became my private life. As I read more, I wrote more – mostly work-related memoranda, letters, and notes in my field journal.

Of course, most of the people I worked with could read French, but they were aliterate; they could, but they did not. My secretary had never read a novel. The Jewish studies teachers had never read a secular book. The general studies teachers had rarely opened anything but textbooks. I visited the homes of doctors and lawyers where there were no bookshelves. When friends visited my home and saw my large personal library, they were shocked. Of course, there were some fascinating exceptions – rabbis with extensive collections of sacred texts, artists who had read many French novels, and a growing population of young Moslems who read newspapers and magazines with the thirst of the desert-parched.

I was showing a filmstrip in Marrakech that demonstrated how a Torah scroll is written by a scribe when one of the frames showed an actual section of the Torah. One little girl in a fourth-grade class immediately recognized the text as coming from a portion she had learned. With great pride, she began to recite the text by heart since the script on the filmstrip was not clear enough to read. The fact that she was a girl was the happy product of the inclusion of females in Moroccan education this past century, but I was also moved by her reading skill, her memory, and her lack of passivity, something I saw way too much of in Moroccan classrooms.

My one attempt at building a school library was not a major success, but by the time I left Morocco, several small libraries had been established in the community. In the FSU, Jewish libraries were our calling card to new communities. We encountered a reading public who loved the world of books. For many in the USSR, books had been the major escape from the grim realities of daily life. One of the ironic successes of the Communist revolution had been to turn a mostly illiterate population into literate Russians, who, in many instances, read their way out of the Soviet Union. For Jews, finding a Jewish book and devouring it was a taste of heaven. A few times I would lend a book to someone on the first day of a conference only to have the person approach me at breakfast the next day, ready to discuss the work he or she had read all night.

In a moving encounter with a senior executive of the Jewish Agency, she told several of us the story of her first Jewish connection. She was at a party in Riga when someone gave her a *samizdat* (underground) copy of Leon Uris's novel *Exodus*. She read it immediately and began her Jewish journey, which involved a difficult immigration to Israel and eventually directing the Jewish Agency office in Moscow. That copy of *Exodus*, which led to her personal exodus, had been smuggled into the USSR in a secret program funded by the JDC, which is why she shared this story with a group of JDC workers.

There are, then, aspects of the different cultures I encountered that can be contrasted to each other, and there are other phenomena which stand alone as testimony to the strangeness I felt in many of these places I visited and worked in.

One of my first tasks in Morocco was to apply some extra funds that the JDC had acquired to upgrading the salaries of the school teachers. Teachers' salaries were abysmally low, and in cooperation with the schools that had to share the burden, the JDC wanted to raise the bar. I was asked by our headquarters in New York to propose a formula for doing so. This was in 1981, before spreadsheets, in an office where we had both 110- and 220-volt outlets (Morocco had had some difficulty in deciding!) and where confusing them led to a burning smell and the loss of our only calculator. Most of my figures were in pencil on large sheets of paper.

Nevertheless, I arrived at a formula after several months of research and a great deal of grade-school arithmetic. It was immediately rejected by New York with the added notice that an expert, who once worked at the New York City Board of Education, would come to help me rewrite the proposal. Although he arrived with no Arabic, French, or Hebrew, he had great expertise in New York salary scales. On his first day, he explained the simple matrix of schooling and experience that establishes all salary grades. "It's simple, Epi. The matrix automatically sets the salary." It was clearly time for him to become acquainted with the realities of North Africa. I accompanied him to several schools and acted as his interpreter, not only of language. He soon found out that most of our teachers had little or no formal schooling. I even had some wonderful principals who had not graduated high school. When we met with one of the school directors to determine how salaries were fixed, he heard of extra payments for a father of many children, less compensation for a smaller class, more money for a henpecked husband, a bit extra for a man who lived in a tiny apartment, a bonus for a circumcision in the family, and so on.

Fortunately, my New York colleague had a fine sense of humor. We became fast friends and he recommended accepting my original proposal. This was my first encounter with the dangers of imposing external models either where they could not possibly fit or where they could be forced to fit, but would end up completely unsuited to local needs.

In the late 1940s and early 1950s the JDC must have "sold" such a model to the remnant French community, which had just been decimated by the German occupation and the Holocaust. Out of eagerness to reorganize French Jewry, France adopted the Federation umbrella model, adapting it to fit the community's needs. The problem was that a model that was suited to individual communities in North America did not work well when transferred to the centrality of Paris in France. This was especially true in the realm of fundraising, where neither the Appel (France's UJA) nor the FSJU (Fonds Social Juif Unifie, the French national equivalent of a local Federation in North America) had any real success in either Paris or the provincial cities. In my years in France, there was one such community of 30,000 Jews which raised $19,000 for the Appel compared to a community of similar size in the United States which raised $5,000,000 for the UJA. The fit was wrong in many ways. A Toulouse businessman did not see why he should write a check to a Parisian fundraiser. The same man could be very generous in his own synagogue, especially if the cause was something concrete and if the fundraising methods were closer to the North African techniques he respected.

In my small synagogue in a village southeast of Paris, one could donate for an aliyah to the Torah to only three charities: synagogue upkeep, a local yeshiva, or KKL (the Jewish National Fund in France). I think very few people in my town gave to the Appel.

I cite this detail from France of the late 1980s in order to illustrate a larger and more complex issue. Whenever we impose exterior models – which are, of course, sometimes necessary – we run the danger of a poor fit, which often is counterproductive. One of my representatives in Siberia was always talking of the religious community versus the secular community, thereby imposing an Israeli model on a much different reality. I met very few Russian Jews who would identify themselves as either secular or religious. It would have been just as ridiculous for me, as a Jew raised in Toronto, to identify Russians or Moroccans as Conservative, Reform, Orthodox, or Reconstructionist. Culture, religion, ethnicity, nationality, and language were confused and confusing categories for new Jews who were searching for an identity that had been brutally stolen.

An even larger question in community organization is one I am struggling with to this day. What is real community? Is it the bureaucratic, centralized, efficient, and effective (especially in fundraising) umbrella which we in North America call the Federation, or is it the warmth and camaraderie one finds in the many small task-oriented groups which are found in Jewish populations of any significant size? At one point in 1992, I made a list of all the Jewish organizations in the brand new community of Cheliabinsk in the Ural mountains: a cultural center, a youth club, a women's federation, an association of Hebrew teachers, a religious community center/synagogue, a Reform religious group, a Zionist organization, an association for Humanistic Judaism, and a repatriation committee. Impressive, *nyet?*

Each one of these small groupings had a purpose-driven ethos that created a real sense of communal belonging, pride, ownership, and even love. One of the groups that grew out of our welfare programs was called *Bayit Cham* (warm home). Several neighbors would meet once a week to share a warm meal cooked by the owner of the largest apartment in the group. I asked a *Bayit Cham* in Novosibirsk in 1997 why they got along so well. Were there truly no fights or differences of opinion? They answered that for years, they had lived isolated and hated by their neighbors. Now that they had found each other they were in constant *simcha* (happiness), which is the Hebrew name they gave their group.

The obvious need for central planning, one charity campaign, budgets, allocation policies, systemic stability, systematic accountability, and strategies for the future creates umbrellas which, by definition, strive for communal unity. While all of this is usually beneficial, as I watched once-great communities disintegrate in North Africa and new ones blossom in the FSU, I often worried about the qualities of diversity, warmth, and smallness that characterize the very groups that umbrella organizations cover.

It is no wonder that our constant mentor, Ralph Goldman, was always admonishing us with the phrase I have quoted elsewhere in this book, "Who appointed you?" from Exodus, chapter 2, verse 14.

At one of the many parties I attended in Morocco, someone offered a local explanation for the custom of clinking glasses before drinking with a friend. The drink is traditionally preceded by a blessing thanking God for all he created, and the drinking itself involves four of the five senses: touch, taste, smell, and vision. Clinking the glasses adds hearing, which completes the full five and makes the blessing fully worthwhile. This almost mythic explanation tells us so much about Moroccan Jews and their God, but also about their pleasure in celebration. I think of it as the North African version of multiple intelligences, way before Harvard and Professor Howard Gardner.

Over the seven years I worked with the Moroccan community, I found that I was influenced by certain aspects of their culture and that my style had been altered somewhat by that influence. For example, after a while I found it difficult to walk from point A to point B without stopping in a café for *un lait cassé* (hot milk with a drop of espresso). My classroom observations in my later years were much more tolerant of the rote recitations and passive students that so disturbed me in my first few months. I noticed in my field notes that speeches made later in my stay were full of Moroccan idiom and carefully concrete. Metaphors were always a problem in Morocco in that the teachers would become obsessed with the concrete example rather than that which was illustrated by the metaphor.

I remember a seminar for teachers in which I was encouraging wall displays and colorful exhibits in the classroom. I spoke of passive learning in which the child indirectly picks up words and ideas that are part of the environment. As an example, I referred to some research that indicated that very young American children could identify the words on the cereal boxes in front of them every morning. At the end of the session, one teacher asked me if the point of the lesson was that Moroccan children should eat American dry cereals in the morning!

Incidentally, when I tried to convince the principal of a new Jewish school in St. Petersburg to put up some beautiful new posters we had created for FSU schools, he objected, claiming that that kind of poster propaganda had no place in post-Soviet education.

However, there were sentiments that I did not share with the local Jews in Morocco because of both my outsider status and my observer's objectivity. Prominent among these was the syndrome I labeled nostalgia-illusion. I can think of one outstanding illustration of this phenomenon among the many instances I encountered. For many years, most large Moroccan communities had a society called *Malbish Arumim* ("He who clothes the naked") to provide clothing and other necessities to the very poor. By the 1980s these functions were all part of the welfare programs supervised by the social agency of the Jewish community (the Communauté Israelite, or C.I.), an umbrella as described above, and partially funded by the JDC. The need was still there, as illustrated by this brief digression.

In one of our summer camps, a little girl from an indigent family hid for ten days the fact that she had arrived without underwear. When our workers quietly went to town and bought her panties, she displayed a smile that I can still see.

Though by 1987, we no longer needed a *Malbish Arumim* society to take care of these kinds of needs, the gentlemen who still guarded the original charter of the society not only wished to continue supplying clothing but also wanted JDC's financial support in order to do so. Even as they admitted that they could no longer raise the money to purchase clothing (there being few Jewish merchants left to donate it from stock), the powerful memories of their former responsibilities persuaded them to suggest the absurd idea that *Malbish Arumim* should replace the anonymous bureaucracy that they identified with the social workers at the C.I.

My dilemma was the tension I referred to above between the efficient umbrella and the warmth of a caring community. Their problem, however, was that they had little touch with the realities of 1987. Their memories stemmed from a period when Jews were both numerous and powerful. Now they were some eight thousand Jews in a country of twenty-five million Moslems, dependent on external aid and lacking strong leadership. The present was so difficult to bear that my friends created from the nostalgia of the past an illusion for the future.

Similar to this was the suggestion by the Ittihad (Alliance Israélite Universelle in Morocco) leadership in the 1990s to build a Jewish university in Casablanca. All of them were so taken by the glorious memories of the *Ecole Normale Hebraique* turning out generations of teachers that the present disintegration forced them to fantasies of a brilliant future that was absurdly unconnected to any real assessment of the situation at hand – nostalgia/illusion.

I could never be judgmental about that sentiment, particularly after I had to face the Jews of Fes when I finally closed down its very last Jewish school due to reduced enrollment. For them I was closing a chapter of Jewish history that had begun long before Maimonides lived there in the twelfth century.

Speaking of Maimonides, both the Moslem intelligentsia and the traditional Jews took pride in his sojourn in Fes from 1160 to 1165. The

Moslems believe that he converted and see him as an Islamic scholar while the Jews, of course, reject that idea and regard Maimonides as a Fassi. I once gave a lift to an old Jerusalem woman, who, when I asked her origins, said that she was from Fes, like the Rambam (Maimonides). The traditional Jews, however, venerate a Maimonides who is quite different from the medieval scholar whose works are studied at the Sorbonne, Harvard, and the Hebrew University. Because of the limited aspects of western culture that the Alliance Israélite Universelle taught the Moroccan Jews, the aspect of the Enlightenment that produced critical scholarship of Jewish sources was completely absent from the Moroccan mentality. While exceptions exist in Paris, Jerusalem, and Montreal – men and women who excel in critical study of their own culture together with scholarly investigation of Moroccan sacred texts and music – most Moroccan Jews were not exposed to this facet of twentieth-century Jewish life. The serving rabbis of my period had no idea that it existed.

Interestingly enough, Jewish studies in the Alliance (Ittihad) schools were not much different from the same disciplines in the Ozar HaTorah or Lubavitch schools. There was no critical method, little teaching of Moroccan Jewish history (not even a textbook devoted to that rich topic), and mostly rote recitation as a pedagogic technique. While the Alliance taught French language, literature, and culture, it left the study of Jewish sources mostly untouched by western thought and preserved in the domain of Moroccan folk religion.

This curricular approach, which resembled that found in Orthodox institutions around the world, did not reflect an ideological position. As noted elsewhere, it was a reflection of the natural religion of the people, undisturbed by events elsewhere in the Jewish world and proud of its own rich heritage.

My experiences in the first months of the Soviet adventure were radically different. Russians were wildly curious readers obsessed with the tools of modernity. If anything, the postmodern tendencies that I had absorbed in my own mid-century education caused me to find the Russians stuck in a modern time warp. I often noted that the best business ventures I could think of developing in the FSU of the 1990s were bowling alleys and drive-in movies! One of the very first educational developments that blossomed in the FSU was the opening of Jewish studies courses (and eventually full departments) in scores of Russian universities. More than that, professors in unrelated fields such as chemistry and mathematics were eager to establish informal study groups to apply their scientific minds to a previously forbidden area of study. Although some of this activity resulted in poor scholarship, all of it was an attempt to read Jewish texts, history, and values back into their lives in ways that they could fathom.

In an earlier chapter, I included a memorandum to headquarters written in November of 1989 immediately after the first meeting of the SUT (Soviet Union Team). That London meeting of seven JDC employees was the very first attempt to organize ourselves into action for a new program in Soviet territory. When I left the JDC in 1999, the SUT met twice a year, once in Jerusalem and once somewhere in the FSU with over sixty workers in attendance. My 1989 memorandum on Jewish education in the USSR, which mostly revealed my ignorance and naiveté, demonstrated how much we were to be surprised by the rapid developments of the next few years.

The apocryphal joke of how I was assigned both the Baltics and Urals/Siberia at the London meeting is that the map was folded; but given how much we knew about the vast USSR, it could have been true. Since the Baltic republics of Estonia, Latvia, and Lithuania were closest to Paris, where I lived, and since many of the cities in the Ural mountains and Siberia were still closed to foreigners, my work began in an area that had been Soviet only since World War II and that was starving for independence.

When I first visited Riga for the JDC in January of 1990, it was actually not my first time in the Latvian capital. I had been there during

Pesach of 1973 on one of those secret missions that at the time I thought were a project of Bnei Akiva (a religious Zionist youth group), but were really an Israeli government operation funded by the JDC. In 1973 I witnessed fear, persecution, and a few brave souls struggling to make aliyah. By early 1990, the Jews were already quite prepared for a radically different future. Some had left, others were planning their departure for Israel, but many had decided that a free Latvia could once again become a home for Jewish life. At least three Jewish organizations were already up and running, the pre-war day school had been re-opened as the first legal Jewish day school in the USSR, and the two Jewish institutions that had survived the Communist period, the synagogue and its matzah factory, were still functioning. Joint ventures (the *perestroika* term for private businesses) were sprouting like spring flowers, and some had already committed themselves to assisting the rebirth of Jewish life in Riga.

That first JDC visit was repeated many times in cities as diverse as Tallinn, Vilna, Kharkov, Cheliabinsk, Omsk, Novosibirsk, Irkutsk, Yakutsk, and Khabarovsk. Sometimes I was one of the first foreigners inside after a closed city such as Perm or Cheliabinsk was opened. At other times I would enter a city soon after its name was changed: Leningrad to St. Petersburg, Sverdlovsk to Ekaterinburg. In Cheliabinsk I was informed after three days of breathing the air that a mission of U.S. volunteers had left minutes after they arrived, having tested that same air and finding it unacceptable. I once asked the head of the Jewish community in Ekaterinburg (Sverdlovsk under the Soviets) what it was like to be in a city whose former name was revived. A top cardiologist in the local hospital and of good humor, she replied that it wasn't clear whether a city is best named after a Jewish Communist general (Sverdlov) or a German courtesan! On my first visit to Kishinev, now Chisinau, I woke up on Shabbat morning to see that all the street signs had been changed from Russian names to new Moldovan names in Latin characters – this after I had memorized the route to the synagogue using Russian street names.

More telling, however, was our surprise at finding and identifying Jews on all of these first visits. We usually entered with a few contacts of names and phone numbers. Within a very short time, sometimes as little as several hours, we were bombarded by Jews who represented every new Jewish organization imaginable; Jewish culture types, synagogue men, Jewish veterans, youth groups, women volunteers, Jewish academics, theater troupes, dance ensembles, and so on. Everyone had a plan, a dream, a property to repatriate and a list of whom not to trust, which usually included the last three people we had met with. The reasons for not trusting another Jewish group ranged from accusations of being a former Communist to being a greedy capitalist joint venturenik.

The one thing no group had was a budget. Even the organizations that had some money and some restored property had neither a budget nor any idea of what a budget was.

It was usually on my second visit to a town that I held a budget preparation seminar. Quite simply, I had to show them what the income side of a ledger looked like. Everyone was an expert at projecting expenses, but the idea of taking responsibility for revenue was novel. The more sophisticated concept of several sources of income was even harder to grasp. The Soviet system did not allow for deficits or creative means for covering them. At one point the State Jewish Museum of Lithuania had twenty paid employees but no building, artifacts, office equipment, or one Yiddish or Hebrew reader. All they really had was expenses.

Equally disturbing to an organizational Jew such as myself was the lack of distinction between lay and professional leadership. Contrary to our expectations and to the many warnings from so-called Soviet experts, we found many Jews who were willing to volunteer their time and even money to Jewish causes such as welfare, synagogue renewal, education, and communal organization. However, many of these volunteers blurred the lines between voluntary communal activity and their respective vocations. For example, businessmen assumed we could connect them to their counterparts in New York. (Not so terrible, I thought, since many

UJA leaders in New York made important business connections through their volunteer work on various boards.) It was when presidents of new communities wanted salaried positions that I started to fret. In some cases, plans were proposed to build a synagogue-cum-shopping centre on reclaimed Jewish property with public capital and an expectation of private profit! Slowly, with forced flexibility on both sides, we arrived at solutions that worked in this new environment.

The saving grace was adaptability. The Soviet system had put up so many obstacles over seventy years of Communist rule that simple citizens had to adapt quickly in order to survive and, in some cases, to flourish. The symbol of this for me was the handbag that every Soviet citizen carried in case some needed item suddenly became available. One night on the Moscow metro I saw a woman "wearing" about fifty rolls of toilet paper. She had obviously come across a supply, strung them together, and was wearing them home. A friend in Novosibirsk explained the food shortages of the early 1990s in the following manner: "No food in the stores, only food at home!" Of course, the famous joke of the Soviet days was, "Whatever food you can't find in the refrigerator, you can find in the radio."

This adaptability resonated with me because of my time in North Africa, where almost nothing changed from decade to decade. Just as I was getting used to working and shopping in dirhams, the Moroccan currency, I noticed that the numbers people were quoting were in the millions, not tens or thousands. What I discovered was that everyone from street vendors to Rabat banking officials used the currency figures of another period, two devaluations back. There were even some souk merchants who used the numbers of a yet earlier currency. The cuisine in Morocco is ancient and well guarded by a very conservative palate. In Russia, which also has its culinary pride, when there are eggs, one gets eggs; when there is kasha, one eats kasha. Whatever was available became the meal, and the very best was made of it.

As soon as *perestroika* and *glasnost* became the reality of late-1980s Soviet Communism, the Jews began to organize as quickly as private business did. Those of us who traveled in Eastern Europe and the Soviet Union during that period noted how rapidly the streets changed. People started selling anything and everything on street corners. A few months later, crude wooden kiosks opened up. Within a short time, the kiosks became permanent aluminum and plastic structures with electric signs, refrigeration, and running water. Soon after that, the kiosks moved into old Soviet government buildings and became boutiques and storefronts.

Of course, the progress of this transition to free capitalism was slower or faster depending on the country, its pre-Soviet history, and who was still in power. Some countries were much better equipped than others for these radical changes. Hungarians could buy an old Tupolev 154 aircraft from Russia and turn it into a Boeing with new upholstery and smiling cabin staff. Ukrainians, on the other hand, could buy a brand new Boeing and, within months, have it look, smell, and operate like an old Aeroflot Tupolev. Not all of this growth was legitimate, and much of it did nothing for the common person, the aged, or the infirm.

There was one aspect of life that post-Soviets and Moroccans seemed to share: a kind of fatalism that pervaded both cultures. In Morocco it stemmed from a combination of Islamic and Jewish folk superstition, while in the FSU it might have come from a kind of tragic pessimism deep in the Russian psyche. I remember being trapped in a Novosibirsk elevator for more than an hour and being the only one of six (in an elevator for four, which might explain the breakdown) who seemed seriously concerned about our fate. One could argue that this incident better illustrates the adaptability I spoke of above, but I think that Russian fatalism is one of the factors behind that adaptability.

During the summer of 1986, while I was vacationing out of country, a young boy died at one of our Moroccan summer camps. The circumstances of the death were problematic, but my staff in Casablanca never called me. Their sense of the situation was that the camper was dead and that there was nothing I could do. Along with concern for the family and the impact on the other children, I was worried about how it had happened, who responded, how effective the response was, and whether the camp was liable. My staff failed to understand my concern and assured me that the family accepted the death of their young child as one accepts lightning and thunder, as an act of God. Liability was never discussed.

One morning my Casablanca office staff informed me that Mme. V. was dying in the Home de Vieux, our wonderful home for the elderly. I knew that this particular resident was a Holocaust survivor from Austria who had somehow ended up in Casablanca after the war. I ran the few blocks to the Home and found the lady in respiratory distress in the building's infirmary section. When I asked for the doctor and whether an ambulance had been ordered, there was shock on the faces of the Home staff. "She's dying." Even without any medical training, I had figured that out and assumed the next step was medical intervention in a hospital (actually in a private clinic, this being Casablanca). "But she's dying," they said. This was becoming inter-planetary communication. I insisted. The ambulance was called and, of course, she died a bit less peacefully in the clinic that afternoon. I had had my lesson in Moroccan fatalism.

One Jewish topic took on new significance for me in both Morocco and the FSU: the Nazi Holocaust. In Morocco, while there was awareness of the destruction that took place in nearby Europe, there was deep gratitude, even reverence, for the role that Mohammed V had played during World War II vis-à-vis the Vichy authorities. He had made it clear that the Jews of Morocco were his subjects and equal to his Moslem citizens. By doing so, he saved the population from internment and possible death. In fact, his tomb in Rabat is a site for Jewish pilgrimage. When an official Jewish delegation arrives, the Moslem reciting Koran leaves and is replaced by a Jew reciting Psalms, and special Jewish hymns are read.

My synagogue in La Varenne, outside of Paris, was an Ashkenazi house of worship before the war, but most of the congregants were killed by the Nazis. On Yom Kippur, when the Casablanca-born rabbi read the list of those killed and their ages, there was a deathly silence among the current congregants, most of whom were North Africans who had arrived after 1945. In memory of the history of the synagogue, I was called up each year to read a hymn that is part of the Ashkenazi High Holiday ritual, but that is not in the Sephardic liturgy.

In a territory where World War II was called the Great Patriotic War, Hitler's destruction of European Jewry was only part of a much larger Russian saga. The memory of the many millions of Soviet citizens and soldiers who were killed or maimed by Hitler's forces was in the forefront of Soviet consciousness and conscience. While the Jews were very much aware of what happened to the millions of Eastern European Jews, they were also emotionally attached to other aspects of the story.

Thousands of Polish Jews fleeing eastward had ended up in various Soviet cities and labor camps along the route of their flight. In Khabarovsk one could talk Warsaw Yiddish to a former tailor and his friends. "Stalin accused me of being a spy. *Vus far a shpion? Ich bin a Varshaver shneider.*" ("What spy? I'm a Warsaw tailor.")

The Jews of Russia were also aware that more than two hundred thousand Jewish soldiers of the Red Army were killed in the war. There was, of course, an element of national pride in this, even though the number was never officially recognized. Worse still, Stalin sought to wipe out all traces of Jewish heroism. Jewish soldiers and officers who were to be decorated for valor and heroism were removed from the lists. In the 1990s, Jewish veteran groups including former high-ranking officers were attempting to rewrite that chapter of Soviet history with the Jewish presence restored to its rightful place.

In those Soviet republics closer to the West, where Hitler's forces were in control, I was taken to many Nazi killing sites: a ravine in town, a field covered over with suburban apartments, or a clearing in the forest.

All of these sites had to be rededicated after the fall of the USSR so that the plaques indicated that Jews, rather than merely Soviet citizens, had been slaughtered.

One of the consequences of the return of Soviet Jews to the corpus of world Jewry and its national memory is the new documentation we now have on the effect of the Holocaust on this part of the Jewish world. While our Shoah scholars knew most of the facts before, the presence among us of aging veterans and the many families who fled eastward has significantly altered our perception of both the scope of the Nazi destruction and Stalin's cover-up of Jewish heroism.

I was especially moved by some of the families I encountered in Siberia who, unlike the stable, centuries-old families of Morocco, were defined by instability and mass movement over many time zones. While the Moroccans could speak of thousands of years in Fes or Marrakech, the FSU Jews spoke of thousands of kilometers of walking. Jews came to Siberia in many waves of internal immigration. Very rarely, I met a descendant of a pre-Soviet merchant family, and the Magen David in the brickwork of the public library of Irkutsk attests to the early presence of a wealthy Jewish merchant who was proud enough of his heritage to include it in the design of his mansion. Of course, there were also prisoners exiled to Siberia by both the Czar and the Soviets. Many of them settled in Siberia after their prison terms and raised their families in their adopted cities. There were loyal Communist Jews who came east to various collective farms and to Birobidjan in fulfillment of Soviet ideology. There were the thousands of Jews who fled eastward during the war, many of whom settled in Siberian cities. Lastly, there were Jewish families who, after the war, realized that their children would not be accepted into the great universities of the western USSR due to the quota system that restricted Jewish enrollment. They moved eastward voluntarily in order to improve their children's chances in the universities of Tomsk, Akademgoradok, and other cities.

All of the Jews accepted their fate of living in this cold climate. Many of them came to love the taiga, the beauty of the birch trees, navigating the great rivers, driving on the winter ice highways, and fishing the magnificent lakes, and they took visible pride in their status as tough Siberians. In fact, the most common question posed to me about aliyah to Israel was whether a Siberian could stand the heat. I never knew if they were referring to the climate, the Palestinian conflict, or both!

There was a brief period soon after the Soviet Union fell in 1991 when the resulting political ambiguity created a great deal of anxiety across the former Soviet territories. I attended a ceremony in the new day school of Tallinn, Estonia at which the children were given their first prayer books, which included a new Russian translation provided by the JDC. I can no longer count how many siddur ceremonies I have attended in Jewish schools around the world, but this one was unique. Handing a prayer book to these children was equivalent to giving their Judaism back to them, their parents, and their grandparents; but it was also creating a new chapter for their own grandchildren. It was one of those moments where the present corrected the past and assured the future. The children sang the popular song to the words of Nachman of Bratslav, "All of the world is a narrow bridge and the main thing is not to fear at all." The Jews of Tallinn, like their brothers and sisters across the FSU, were living on a very narrow bridge and were demonstrating great courage in place of fear: courage to uproot and move to Israel, courage to stay and recreate a Jewish life – the kind of courage and pride that inspired all of us who came into contact with them.

Marc Chagall, who was born in Vitebsk in 1887, was educated in a cheder (private Jewish studies classroom) in the strong Jewish community of that city. By the end of the nineteenth century, seventy-two percent of the Jewish children in Vitebsk studied in a variety of Jewish schools. The Jewish streets of Vitebsk included Chasidim, mitnagdim (opponents of Chasidism), Bundists, and fervent Zionists. Chagall left the shtetl of

Vitebsk physically, but characters from that community ended up on the ceiling of the Paris Opera, which he painted much later in his life.

In the first quarter of the twentieth century, Shlomo Matusof was also born in Vitebsk. He studied in a clandestine Chabad yeshiva in Moscow, hidden from the Soviets and funded by the Joint. Eventually, he became a Chabad emissary to Morocco and spent over fifty years of his life in the service both of his spiritual master, the Rebbe, and the Jews of Morocco. Two gentlemen of Vitebsk who each learned French, but for very different reasons!

Here are two vastly different people, a painter and an educator, each a creative genius in his own sphere. Each one absorbed the cultures of their blended, formative environments. Chagall could no more abandon the shtetl in him while living in bohemian Paris than Matusof could forget the Russian he learned so well in a Soviet labor camp, his punishment for studying forbidden texts. One morning in Casablanca when I needed real news about a terrorist attack the day before in Jerusalem, it was Rabbi Matusof who had the information. He had listened to BBC's Russian broadcast the preceding night on his short wave radio. Both men came from the same place and ended up on very different journeys. One entered the western world of art and culture, but proudly displayed the side of him that was tied to the shtetl. Another openly defied the defining culture of his country to maintain loyalty to his Jewish values and practices. He used his personal experience of clashing cultures to work among Jews who were so different from him and his Russian origins.

While I'm not sure that my Moroccan friends could identify with these cultural tensions, since they have experienced cultural unanimity and stability over the last many centuries, the Russian Jews I encountered understood and identified with this struggle between worldviews.

Once, at a staff meeting with invited guests from the Vaad (the first post-Communist Russian Jewish umbrella organization), comparisons were being made with American Jewish identity. One of the Vaad leaders exploded in sociological fury, stating that in this domain, Russian Jews have nothing in common with American Jews. Americans can be both American and Jewish, but a Jew cannot be and will never be a Russian.

To digress a bit, I heard of another major difference between Americans and Russians from a St. Petersburg intellectual. He told me that if an American doesn't want to do something, he fakes a headache. On the other hand, if a Russian is in a similar situation, he gets a real headache!

In Vladivostok one evening I was being entertained by a very wealthy "new Russian" businessman, a Jew married to a gentile woman with two children whom he had sent to America for private schooling. The boy, aged fifteen, was asking me in prep-school English who he was – a Jew or a Russian. I explained that he was born a Soviet, educated partly in the U.S., now back in Vladivostok. He could choose his future, but I saw in his face that the choice was one laden with angst and cultural ambiguity. His sister, who was sixteen, asked me when I was leaving. When I answered that I would be leaving on Wednesday, she expressed her disappointment. "If you stayed longer, you could have made us a Shabbat."

One of the old Warsaw tailors living in Khabarovsk, delighting in his long-lost Yiddish, explained the process in a cryptic phrase that requires decoding: *"Der Zhid iz gevoren a Yid!"* The Jew (stigmatized by the label "Zhid") has become a Jew, now newly proud of the label, "Yid."

At times I thought of smelly cheese that suddenly becomes haute cuisine when one encounters the rich taste. The stink is replaced by an appreciation of the culture, the tradition, and the competent transmission of the art of cheese-making over generations.

As the Jews of the FSU became exposed to the language and the literature of the Jewish people and to the many voices of contemporary Jewry both in Israel and in the Diaspora, they joined the search of all modern Jews for their place under the sun. I found myself smiling as some Jews rallied to Chabad Chasidism, with its missionary zeal, while others passionately rejected it; as some Jews were immediately convinced of aliyah while others decided to stay under difficult conditions; as some Jews found a spiritual home in the Reform movement while others saw it as inauthentic or irrelevant. And it wasn't only the Jews who were searching in the Jewish world.

Because of the high rate of intermarriage among Soviet Jews, there were some non-Jews who had, through one connection or another, not only aligned themselves with the Jewish people but, in some cases, assumed leadership roles. The Jewish studies teacher in Cheliabinsk, the young Burati Talmudist/Hebraist in Ulan Udeh, the synagogue lady in Perm, the Hebrew teacher in Yakutsk at 62 degrees North, and the singer of Bialik poems in Dnieperpetrovsk were among the non-Jewish spirits who were leading the renewal of Jewish life in their respective communities. Whether they were halachically Jewish or not, I always suspected that these souls were with the rest of us at Mount Sinai.

While there can be valid speculation about the future of Moroccan Jewish culture and religion in the twenty-first century, the map is mostly drawn. Israel, France, and Quebec are the main loci and the mix of secularism, multi-culturalism, ethnicity, anti-Semitism, Islamic fundamentalism, and Israeli politics will result in some balance that preserves some aspects of North African culture and erases others. The same speculation about the vast numbers of FSU Jews and their cultural and spiritual identity in the twenty-first century is much more complex.

The mix of intellectual curiosity and great adaptability bodes well for this heterogeneous sub-group of Jews who are now spread across the globe. In many lectures on my experiences with North Africa and the FSU, I referred in ecological terms to the former as a rain forest of the Jewish people and to the latter as a polluted river. The rain forest has its secrets hidden in the beauty of its foliage; some of them remedies for diseases that we continue to suffer. The river has the power to regenerate and cleanse itself. The latter process is in full swing. In Israel, North America, Germany, and many other smaller tributaries, FSU Jews are discovering themselves as Jews and creating a Jewish culture unique to their own past history and present needs.

In many cases, the cultural manifestations of these new Jews in established communities will be somewhat peculiar in the eyes of the "native" Jews. What does a Reform Temple in Toronto have in common with the rituals of Mountain Jews from the Caucasus? Does a Yom ha-Shoah ceremony in New Jersey give voice to the World War II sacrifices of Soviet Jews? Will Pushkin be taught in Israeli schools? Do chess and ballet have their place in Jewish day schools in Germany? How will Israeli politics deal with Russian voters?

While a memoir such as this can have no pretensions of prediction, my experiences in Siberia and other parts of the former Soviet territories lead me to believe that "The Russians are coming!" I think a great part of twenty-first century Jewish life in both Israel and the Diaspora will be written by this new limb of our body.

In Budapest, I attended a production of *La Bohème* with a group of visiting Jewish educators. I had arranged for the Jerusalem Fellows, senior educators from around the world who were studying in Jerusalem, to witness the rebirth of Jewish life in Eastern Europe. One evening, we went to the opera. After the production I asked one of the educators, an Italian, what he thought of the performance. He had seen better, but he wanted to tell us a *La Bohème* anecdote. He once attended a production of this opera in a concert hall that was very poorly heated. The audience was beginning to suffer when Rodolfo sang the aria, "Che gelida manina" (How cold your hands are), to Mimi in the first act. Immediately, someone from an upper balcony shouted in Italian, "Not as cold as our feet!" I found this story intriguing as a metaphor for Jewish literacy.

Most of us who attend the opera think of it as a piece of elite culture where we must be polite, well-behaved, quiet, and well-dressed. We forget its roots as popular entertainment, the equivalent of rock music or rap today. We also do not know the language. Except for a few well-known arias, the music is not ingrained in our souls. Even if we had an issue with a line we understood from the surtitles, we would never shout. But if we were completely at home in the culture, knew the language, had the music coursing through our veins, and were comfortable enough to discern and dissent when necessary, we would. So it is with Jewish literacy. Mere identity is not sufficient to make us worthy of our name, Yisrael, the one who struggles with God. As FSU Jews find their natural place among us and as they learn the language (and most of them have already done a better job at learning Hebrew than the rest of us), they will gather the power to assert themselves as vociferously and as passionately as Jews must.

Without a drop of condescension, I can state that they are already well on the way.

A lay leader of the Alliance Israélite Universelle was giving a speech in Paris about the history of that glorious institution when he noted that a revolution had taken place within the ideology of the AIU. It had originally been established as a beachhead of the French Empire that was designed to bring French culture and *politesse* to the unwashed Jews of the Maghreb and other parts of the Mediterranean basin. Even between the two wars, it saw its mission in France to transform the recently-arrived *"Juifs"* from Eastern Europe into *"Israelites,"* worthy citizens of the Republic. Now, in a very different Europe, the AIU had radically changed its mission to that of Jewish literacy. Even Moroccan Jews, who had centuries of natural Judaism behind them, needed to renew their knowledge of Jewish life in order to deepen their literacy and thereby ensure their future.

I met an old professor in Akademgoradok, the university city near Novosibirsk, who had written a commentary on the Biblical book, Kohelet (Ecclesiastes) many years before the end of Communism. He used the Hebrew of his youth in Poland and long hours of secret scholarship to produce a book that could not be published in Soviet Russia. Now, a former student of his who had become wealthy in the first years after *Perestroika* had published his book, and the slim volume had become a symbol of all that was possible for Russian Jews to become in this new world they inhabited.

The JDC opened a summer camp in Szarvas, Hungary together with the Lauder Foundation and the Jewish Agency. While it began under Communism (albeit the "Goulash Communism" of Hungary) and, at first, served only the children of that country, by the 1990's it was bringing in children from all over Eastern Europe and the FSU. I even sent children from Siberia who spent as much time on train travel as they did at the camp.

In the summer of 1992, there was a group of campers from Czechoslovakia in attendance for one of the two-week sessions. The Hebrew song that was most popular that summer at camp was *Am Echad, Lev Echad* (one nation, one heart). The ritual at Szarvas on the final night of camp was a group of skits put on by each country's group, followed by the anthems of each country and ending with "Ha-tikva," the Israeli national anthem. When the Czechs stood to sing their anthem, they noted that their country was being split into two republics and they were not sure who they were at that point in time. Lots of laughter. They then spontaneously started to sing *Am Echad, Lev Echad* as their anthem and were soon joined by all the other campers.

When I was told this story, I realized that all the artificial national borders that separate Moroccan Jews from Canadian ones, Russian Jews from Israelis, French Jews from Azerbaijanis, or American Jews from Hungarian ones have almost no effect on us as a people. While our various environments have certainly given us different cultural traits, the connective tissue that links us to one another as a unique people is a far greater force than we ever imagined. As the world continues to shrink through communications technology, this unity becomes ever more powerful.

CHAPTER SEVEN

THREE SIBERIAN COMMUNITIES

THIS MEMO TO Asher Ostrin, the director of JDC operations in the FSU, is illustrative of field trips to Siberian communities. While some of the material is repetitive of descriptions elsewhere in the book, I thought it useful to see some of the community issues as first recorded in a field report.

MEMORANDUM

To: Asher

From: Epi

Date: November 27, 1997

Re: Trip Report – November 16–25, 1997

This was a trip to Novosibirsk, Krasnajarsk, and Yakutsk. I traveled with our field representative, Shmuel Levin, and Rabbi Joe Schonwald of the Rochlin Foundation accompanied us to the first two cities.

NOVOSIBIRSK: I am happy to report that we are finally achieving real results in the Novosibirsk community. After seven years of disappointment (mainly due to poor local leadership) we now have a local worker (Alia Alchova), an excellent relationship with the local REK (Yefim Shtallvosser), and a functioning synagogue committee (Boris Malisov). Things turned around for us and the community once we decided to completely ignore our one-time welfare coordinator, a person who gave us lots of anguish.

We rented a small apartment for the community and synagogue use. It is in the center of town and is used for Shabbat programs, community meetings, a youth group, welfare coordination, etc. We contribute $300/month and the local REK contributes $200/month.

The REK people and our coordinator sponsored a Tishrei party. The JDC paid nothing. Local businessmen invested about $2,000. There was an auction which raised a million rubles, the money then donated to a local woman who needs an eye operation. The program included talks about the Tishrei holidays, Israeli dance, Jewish songs, a Sholom Aleichem play, lots of food, etc.

The Monday morning we arrived in Novosibirsk we were asked to come to the community apartment for tefillot. A rabbi had arrived for a few days and Boris Malisov arranged a minyan. I led *shacharit* and Rabbi Joe read Torah. The few synagogue souls in Novosibirsk are slowly getting organized. There is kosher Israeli salami available in supermarkets. Our last day in town Boris and Yefim took us to a local baker who is interested in opening a matzah factory. JDC will help with the initial consultation on condition that we can purchase at a discount.

We had lunch twice on Tuesday because we visited the first two bayit cham apartments in town. In each apartment there were eight neighbors sharing a meal cooked by the apartment owner with JDC-supplied food. The meals were dairy, delicious, and beautifully served. At the second one I jokingly asked if it's always so friendly. Don't they have the occasional fight? There was a moment of laughter, and then one of them said that they used to live unaccepted by their Russian neighbors. Now they found a family and the name of the group explains why they never fight. They call themselves "Simcha." A lady who was celebrating her seventy-first birthday that day told us that she lived all her years in Novosibirsk and never knew there were other Jews in town. Now she found her own family and she is so proud to be a part of it. I never heard better definitions of community.

Tuesday evening we met with a newly-formed Hillel group. I was hoping to call my Siberian student groups Shammai, just for the hell of it, but Yossi Goldman beat me to it. One of the kids played violin. He's a master violinist completely at home with his instrument. When he started playing Jewish melodies he began to improvise and took those tunes to musical places they had never been before. I couldn't help but comment that that is our wish with regard to their Judaism. We want them to become virtuoso Jews, so comfortable with their Judaism that they can improvise and take it to new places; creativity, not continuity. Joe Schonwald appreciated both the dignified care in the bayit cham and the enthusiastic optimism of the Hillel students.

Novosibirsk, with about fifteen thousand Jews, seems to be on the right path to some form of Jewish community life.

KRASNAJARSK: Friday was one of those days of great contrast in Krasnajarsk. After a preliminary meeting with two women who run the welfare operation, Shmuel and I went to a home visit. I was expecting the usual situation, an old pensioner, a run-down apartment, a sad story somewhat alleviated by our food parcels and visits. Instead I was put in shock by a story so devastating that I broke down later in the hallway. (A sad first!) We met an aging grandmother with her own heart condition caring for a nine-year-old epileptic with some form of partial paralysis. Her divorced daughter, the child's mother, lives in the apartment with her own case of epilepsy and some other nervous disorder. The grandmother is constantly fighting with the daughter and caring for the child. The child has several large seizures a month despite the best Russian medications. It was a desperate situation with absolutely no remedy. The community helps with food parcels and some equipment. We will purchase a new tape recorder – the child loves music and has never been to school. He doesn't talk but communicates in grunts. I had the overwhelming feeling that this child was far more ill than he needed to be. In another setting he might be talking and walking normally and have the epilepsy under control. Aliyah is the only solution, but I'm sure JAFI will reject this family for obvious reasons. This visit was one of my lowest moments in JDC, feeling both their tragedy and my helplessness.

Friday night, Rabbi Joe, Shmuel, and I went to daven in the Krasnajarsk shul. I had been there twice before to see a wreck of an old building with no heat and no proper lighting, broken walls, splintered furniture, etc. With the help of many thousands of dollars donated by a local non-Jew, Yasha Brill built the model of a small town synagogue: beautiful woodwork, creative design, intimate atmosphere, real light, and a sound heating system. If anyone in JDC wants to see a model shul building for a community of two thousand Jews, Krasnajarsk is the city to visit. One defect tells an old story about Siberia. Jews who came to Siberia from Poland and Ukraine didn't know much, but they knew that one prayed facing east. It's always hard to tell the old-timers that east of Moscow one faces west for prayer. Fortunately, the interior furnishings can be turned around before the gala dedication in a few weeks.

From the pits of despair Friday morning to the beauty of Kabbalat Shabbat in a new Siberian synagogue! Rabbi Joe led the service and treated everyone to Carlebach melodies. Reb Shmaya, the visiting Chabad rabbi who is close to this community, was also in town and very proud of the local achievement.

Yasha Brill is the local leader; one very powerful and creative Buncher graduate. He will probably err with the celebrations surrounding the dedication of the new synagogue. He is involving too many local dignitaries and turning it into much too grandiose an affair. As it happens, JDC will not be present (not intended), and that's probably for the better. All the same, Yasha has done some wonderful work in this community. When he makes aliyah, the gap will be hard to fill.

The rest of our visit was given over to the usual meetings with local communities. Krasnajarsk was the only Siberian town to sponsor a Jewish Book Festival. It was held in a local ethnic culture centre and was a major success; both internally and vis-à-vis the general population. An interesting by-product was Shmuel's insistence that the festival be jointly sponsored by all community organizations. That created real community cohesion and showed Yasha how to "play well with others."

Krasnajarsk is the base of our Siberia-Vostok operations and as soon as we get proper accreditation, we will open up a real office.

YAKUTSK: I think Shmuel and I made a bit of JDC history at 2:00 AM on Monday, November 24, 1997 when we landed in Yakutsk. I imagine we were the first JDC staff to ever set foot in this 62nd-parallel town of two hundred thousand people. About five hundred Jews reside in this frozen piece of real estate. Yakutia, the province, is larger than India. It has gold, diamonds, oil, gas, some very poor people, and a lot of dilapidated houses. The permafrost is 350 meters deep. Houses are built on concrete stilts and if the frost melts too much in the summer, the house falls down. (As Dave Barry says, this actually happens!) When we arrived the town went into a fortunate warm spell of about minus 28 degrees centigrade. It had been minus 42 degrees centigrade a day before. This is one cold dump of a place that can only go up – and will!

Sarah Lifshitz is the head of the community that registered itself in 1991. Misha and Elena Gurevich are the most active members. Misha runs everything and Elena, his non-Jewish wife, teaches Hebrew and directs the Sunday school. They live in a log cabin. (I'm not making any of this up.)

Interestingly enough, the first place they took us was the Jewish cemetery, a completely separate burial ground near the centre of town. There are some very old graves with poetic Hebrew inscriptions, but there was so much snow, it was hard to uncover too many stones. They loved the custom of washing hands after being in a cemetery that I taught them, but we did it in the snow. It was less cold than the water which comes from melted river ice that they cut off in blocks and melt in the house. (I'm still not embellishing!) The community pays an old woman to live in a hut in the cemetery to guard and tend it. It was in her hut that I came to realize how important this cemetery is for these Yakutsk Jews. They have no Jewish memories at all. One eighty-year-old told me he last heard Yiddish in 1924 when his grandmother died. Every Jew is buried in the cemetery, without any ritual, but in a Jewish place. He joins his ancestors who had Jewish memories. It's also possible that local Shamanism, which reveres holy ground, has had some effect on these Jews. Of course, they asked for some JDC help in maintaining the place. I will send some minimal assistance, but I also intend to send someone to teach them some Jewish burial and mourning rituals along with a supply of shrouds. By the way, to bury someone in permafrost you have to heat the ground with huge flames for an entire day.

We spent one full day and two nights in Yakutsk, most of it talking to Sarah and Misha while we visited a geological museum and a permafrost laboratory deep underground; the latter directed by an active member of the community. Another active Jew is currently running for mayor. In the evening we met with several Jews and discussed welfare, education, the cemetery, the Sunday school of thirty children, and community holiday celebrations – all this in Misha's log cabin.

I want to give Yakutsk a Pesach it won't forget. I intend to ask Jonathan Porath for a special student group to lead a Seder and teach. I will supplement the budget to provide special food. Yakutsk deserves the same Seder that others had six years ago.

Misha's daughter is on Naaleh-16 and the whole family will eventually leave. For now, he and Sarah are providing strong leadership in a tiny community that will get the JDC attention it deserves. We will stay in phone contact and Shmuel will visit once a year. Sakhalin and Kamchatka are next….

CHAPTER EIGHT

RELIGION AND SPIRITUALITY

IN THE EARLY 1970S I was a member of Chavurat Shalom, a spiritual community in Boston that in the anti-establishment fashion of the time stressed study, prayer, community, and the personal spiritual quest. Some of what we did was a bit radical for the time (now quite tame in retrospect), but has since been copied many times over by Jewish groups searching for meaning and values within and beyond the standard North American denominational settings. There was some resistance at the time, and I have a vividly hilarious memory of a member of a Conservative synagogue berating me for belonging to that group that changed the melody of Ein Keloheinu, a hymn chanted at the end of Shabbat morning services. My reaction was laughter at the thought that the melody she knew as her symbol of eternal Jewish tradition was in fact that of a German drinking song.

Years later, both in North Africa and in the FSU, I came to appreciate the force of that complaint, having witnessed what music and liturgy meant for a folk religion steeped in ancient traditions. On the negative side, the opposite, I realized what a vacuum had been created by the

Soviet repression, which cut three generations off from the melodies of the Jewish soul.

I am reminded of a story I heard in Israel about the cantorial concert that was once a regular Saturday afternoon program on Israeli radio. The religious authorities managed to get the program cancelled on the grounds that it was a violation of Shabbat. The next week in the Knesset, a very secular, Communist member of parliament complained that the rabbis and their political parties had robbed him of his *oneg Shabbat*, his Sabbath pleasure, by canceling the program of cantorial music, which he had loved since his childhood in Europe.

One Ramadan night in Casablanca, my wife and I were watching King Hassan II pray on television (there wasn't much else to watch!), and I was surprised to note that the melody he chanted was very similar to one that was used for a particular prayer in the synagogues down the street. However, I couldn't be overly surprised since years before, I had noticed how much the Armenian church music I loved was so reminiscent of certain Eastern European cantorial melodies. So while musicologists can easily argue about the give and take of centuries of melodic interaction and coexistence, the music of the Moroccan synagogue was and is an essential part of the spiritual heritage of all Moroccan Jews.

How many times have I spent a Shabbat in an Israeli hotel when the Moroccans on vacation have taken over the hotel synagogue with the force of their musical memories? Once, when a Torah reader could not be found, a tourist who had just donned a kippa to enter the synagogue read from memory with no mistakes in pronunciation, punctuation, or musical notation from a Torah scroll that contained none of them. (The parchment scroll used for ritual reading has only consonants – no vowels, punctuation, or musical notation.)

While interviewing a candidate in Moscow for the six-month Hebrew University course for Jewish educators, one young man, explaining his Jewish awakening, told us he was a classical musician with a very low tolerance for kitschy Jewish music. A friend had invited him to a concert of just such fare and he accepted against his better judgement. He found himself surprised that the music touched a chord in his soul, and that was the beginning of his reconnection to Jewish life.

What became clear over the full eighteen years of fieldwork was the powerful effect that the spiritual life had in its everyday presence in Morocco and the devastating lack of Jewish spirituality among our folk in the vast territory of the former Soviet Union. Let me use Shabbat as the first illustration of this.

Like all other aspects of religion, Shabbat was a natural part of the life of most Moroccan Jews. Like most other Jews of the twentieth century, the urban Jews of late twentieth-century Morocco had made their peace with the business and leisure demands of modern society, but Shabbat remained a significant part of the weekly schedule. Friday was very much a day of preparation and one could easily spot the maids of Jewish families carrying the unbaked Shabbat breads and the pots of *dafina* (the Moroccan version of Ashkenazi *cholent* or Yemenite *hamin* for a hot Shabbat lunch) to the street ovens. On Friday night the synagogues of Casablanca, Fes, Meknes, Rabat, Tanger, and Marrakech were full. One early Saturday morning, unable to sleep, I ventured out on my balcony and thought I heard a synagogue service, but it was way too early. Checking with a local rabbi later, I found out that indeed, there was a dawn service of men, who opened their shops on Shabbat out of commercial necessity, but still wanted to pray together before publicly desecrating the holiness of the day. I knew many Jews who drove to the beach Saturday on afternoons but never would have considered doing so before the long Shabbat morning services followed by the *dafina* meal.

Most of the youth groups and summer camps were organized by French-oriented agencies such as the DEJJ (Departement Educatif de la Jeunesse Juive) and the Scouts (EIM – Eclaireurs Israelites du Maroc). There is no doubt that the original purpose of this youth work was to bring the poor Jewish children of the mellah closer to French culture, as I illustrate elsewhere in the book. However, Shabbat at camp was a totally

Interior of renovated Omsk Synagogue
with locally carved *aron kodesh*.

Interior of renovated Omsk Synagogue
with locally carved *aron kodesh*.

Seymour Epstein and Asher Ostrin at the dedication
of the Omsk Synagogue, December, 1995.

natural event, organic to the spirit of both the children and their leaders. It was not imposed on the campers either by religious coercion or as a curricular objective. It was simply a product of their usual custom. Shabbat was descriptive, not prescriptive, and the Shabbatot that I spent in these camps were some of the most inspiring spiritual experiences I ever knew because of the all-encompassing atmosphere – the music, the food, and the authentic sincerity of it all.

Then I think back to my first Shabbat in Moscow in 1989. The Choral Synagogue on Arkhipova Street was one of two for the hundreds of thousands of Jews living in this large metropolis. No matter, since there was very little demand on any day except Simchat Torah and Passover Eve. The synagogue was shabby, dirty, smelly, and bereft of anything even approaching music. Yet, when the few old men started muttering the service, I felt at home. I sensed a connection to my own past, which was more immediate than the sentiment I had grown to feel for the Moroccan rites I had learned in North Africa. The little bit of melody I heard was my melody. The Hebrew sounded like that of my father and grandfather.

Again, the little that there was in Riga, Vilna, and Odessa was an echo from my Ashkenazi past. However, it was in Siberia that I saw the full spiritual devastation of a people without sacred time. My first Shabbat in Khabarovsk was such a shock. Being so far east, Shabbat comes to Khabarovsk much before it arrives anywhere else in the Jewish world, way before Jerusalem, Casablanca, or Toronto. Shabbat, however, arrived for many decades in Khabarovsk completely unnoticed. In the early 1990s, only a few Jews of the ten to fifteen thousand in the city had heard about Shabbat from an elderly grandparent, a visit to Moscow, or a visiting Christian missionary who wanted to show them the Shabbat that Jesus observed. However, most of the Jews in town had never heard of any Jewish day except Passover, entered a synagogue or read a Jewish book. Even the seven-day week was not a reality for most, whose Soviet work schedule arranged the week without a real weekend. Holidays were

Soviet events that most people privately mocked but faithfully observed for the leisure time that they provided. Any notion of a sacred twenty–five-hour period of spiritual rest and recreation, which repeats itself weekly, was not part of the planet these Jews inhabited.

Nevertheless, the thirst for knowledge of such sacred moments in our tradition was evident everywhere. While it was clear that the strictures of a halachic Shabbat were not an option for most of these people, their desire to taste and know Shabbat and the rhythm of the Jewish calendar was ubiquitous. (This was not so different from the Moroccans described above, except for the ignorance caused by the Soviet rupture.) One sensed this thirst in the speed at which synagogues were restored, libraries built, schools of all types opened, and courses of Jewish studies initiated at universities across the breadth of the FSU. Although Khabarovsk had no synagogue building, by 1997 there were regular Friday evening services led by young people and attended by elderly Warsaw Jews with memories.

One poignant Shabbat story in the Ural Mountains stayed with me. We were at Saturday lunch in a local apartment and I had made the blessing over wine after having prayed alone in my hotel room, there being no synagogue in Cheliabinsk at the time. I was sitting with a devoted volunteer from a kibbutz in Israel, who had come to teach Hebrew. A young woman was telling the rest of us that she had spent a traditional Shabbat in Moscow at some religious institution recently opened, and that she was especially moved by *havdala*, the ceremony using a candle, wine, and spices to end Shabbat on Saturday night. She begged her Hebrew teacher, the kibbutznik, to perform the ceremony for her right then and there. He quietly admitted to me that in all his fifty years on a secular kibbutz he had never seen *havdala*. He asked me to do it for them instead. I explained that I would gladly do it and was intending to do so anyway, but only at the end of Shabbat, many hours later. Of course, neither the Russian Jews at lunch nor my kibbutznik friend could fathom why I wouldn't immediately give this young woman her wish.

The holidays of the Jewish year were also a part of the natural rhythm of life in Morocco. Preparations for Sukkot began much before the festival with the building of sukkot in courtyards and on rooftops. Since many of the poorer residents lived in apartment buildings, one courtyard sukka was used in shifts by many families eating rushed meals or in some cases, using the sukka just for the preliminary blessings with the rest of the meal eaten indoors. Most surprising to me was the vast number of etrogim (citrons, one of the four species used ritually in Sukkot prayers) available and their low cost, since they grow in southern Morocco. In most Jewish communities one purchases a single etrog at great cost – Eastern European folklore is full of stories about the effort to obtain a single etrog to serve an entire community. In Casablanca, a crate of etrogim was brought to my office and I was encouraged to take as many as I wanted. The less desirable ones were even used as decorations in the sukkot I visited.

At a certain point in the spiritual development of FSU communities, we made the decision to ship the four species needed for Sukkot prayers to select communities; usually those with a functioning synagogue. This involved much planning in June and July for a festival that occurs in September–October. The logistics of shipping these fragile and cumbersome plants in a territory with no organized transport were overwhelming. In some cases, they arrived well before the holiday and spoiled too soon while in others, they arrived well after Sukkot. In many instances, they came to communities where not a single soul knew their purpose. One man in Irkutsk reshipped a set to a friend in Omsk who had not seen an etrog in fifty years and wept at the sight of it. Another man, notified of its imminent arrival by our Moscow office, asked whether it was 110 or 220 volts! Our shipments of pre-fabricated sukkot were also a mixed blessing, since none of them were built to withstand the early snows of Siberia.

The synagogue in Alibag, India (one of the original Bene Israel villages) has in its garden a citron tree, a palm, a myrtle, and a willow. It is probably the only synagogue in the world that grows its own four Sukkot species. Regrettably, there are not enough Jews left in Alibag to hold proper services on a regular basis.

For various reasons, Passover was the best-known holiday in the USSR. Most of the celebrations consisted of finding matzot in one way or another and using them to bring the ancient celebration of freedom into homes where freedom was only a luxurious dream. When we entered the Soviet Union in 1989, we found several functioning matza bakeries that usually began production in a synagogue basement in January and produced enough matzot for the Jews in the immediate vicinity. None of these bakeries operated under rabbinic supervision and the matzot produced were probably not kosher by Orthodox standards. However, given their function as the sole reminder of the potential for delivery from slavery to freedom and given the superhuman efforts required to bake them, these matzot might have been the most pleasing to God on high.

I met a matza hero in Irkutsk on my first visit in 1990. Mordecai L. was already in his eighties when I met him on one very cold morning in the synagogue. This was the original Irkutsk synagogue, but by 1990 the lower floor had been turned into a factory and the upper floor, which had previously been the women's balcony, was now the entire synagogue. Every morning, Mordecai, a pensioner, would open the synagogue, don his tallit and tefillin and recite the morning prayers alone. On Shabbat he would attract a few old men to join him. As he explained all this to me over a welcome glass of hot tea, he decided to offer me the opportunity of a lifetime. He brought me to the machine he had crafted to bake matzot, a Rube Goldberg collection of metal parts and wires. He had assumed that I had come to live in Irkutsk as a JDC worker (He knew the Joint's work from World War II.), and he informed me that since he was making aliyah, I could now assume the responsibility of matza baker for all of Siberia. He produced a portfolio of letters, both requesting matzot and thanking him for timely delivery from across several time zones (we should have used him at Sukkot!), and then he told me the secret of his success.

It seems that several decades before, the Soviet commissar for the Irkutsk region died. The next morning, his widow appeared at the synagogue looking for Mordecai. She explained that she wanted a Jewish burial for her husband, whom she had learned was Jewish on his deathbed the previous day. Mordecai immediately grasped the opportunity and said that he could provide this complicated service if she, with her party connections, could provide him with an annual delivery each December of twenty tons of flour and a great deal of wrapping paper for postal delivery. They each carried out their respective parts of the deal, and the Siberian Jews had matzot every year since.

By the way, the paper shortage in Siberia, which is surrounded by forests, must have been a longstanding problem, since we have evidence of it from an amazing document found in an Irkutsk archive. There was a rabbi still serving in Irkutsk in the 1930s who wanted to write a commentary on the Torah but could find no paper. He stole into the local Red Army firing range and "liberated" old targets, on which he wrote his circular commentary. Perhaps it was the inspiration derived from such spiritual resistance which kept the Irkutsk synagogue functioning for decades after.

It was a bad moment when I told Mordecai that I was leaving Irkutsk in two days, but the JDC subsequently took on a major responsibility in the procurement of flour for existing bakeries, the shipping of matzot to areas without bakeries, and the opening of new bakeries in certain key cities.

A colleague of mine who was visiting an elderly woman in her apartment in some Ukrainian city noted the obvious poverty that qualified her for welfare assistance supported by the Joint. There was very little furniture, almost no food, and the usual decrepit surroundings. In the midst of this squalor, he noticed a large feather on a bare shelf and asked the woman about it. Shocked that an informed Jew would not

Mordechai with his baking machine.   Mordechai with his matzot.

Mordechai, the matza baker of Irkutsk, 1990s.

know, she explained that it was for *bedikat chametz*, the annual ritual of searching for forbidden leavened products on the day before Passover eve. That feather was her one and only ritual object and she cherished it like a crown jewel.

In our attempt to help Jews back to the Jewish people, we decided that communal Passover sedarim could establish an important link between a holiday most had heard about and a future of deeper knowledge and positive identity. Of course, the seder theme of slavery to freedom was a motif that resonated with the times we were living through. My personal experiences with these sedarim in Novosibirsk, Odessa, and Riga were so powerfully intense that verbal description does them no credit. It is sufficient to point out that certain phrases from the *Haggada* (the prayers, legends, and songs recited at the Passover seder) rang as true as when they were originally written.

Blessed be He who keeps His promises to Israel....

In every generation, all people should regard themselves as if they came forth out of Egypt.

Blessed are You, O Lord... who has redeemed us... and brought us to this night....

This is the day that the Lord has made; let us rejoice and be glad thereon.

Ritual became reality, and the primal force of the poetry was evident in everyone's face.

The first communal seder in Novosibirsk in 1990 was held in a rented hall used for private parties. We provided some wine, grape juice, matzot, the ingredients of the ritual seder plate, Russian *haggadot*, and an Israeli volunteer couple to lead the seder. The locals added apples, boiled

Pesach seder in Riga, 1990.

Pesach seder in Riga, 1990.

potatoes, vodka, and brandy. While the last two items were not exactly kosher for Passover, the locals added them to make the event a celebration in Russian terms. The next morning I was on a long walk with the president of the community in order to attend Passover services in a tiny log synagogue on the outskirts of Novosibirsk. He told me that the staff at the rented hall had been shocked at one aspect of the event the evening before. By the end of the seder, most of the vodka and brandy were still in the bottles. The recitation of prayers, the story of the exodus from Egypt, and the singing so moved the two hundred participants that they had forgotten to drink. Such a thing had never happened in that Russian hall before!

Traditionally, we recognize the first Passover as *Pesach shel Mitzrayim*, the Egyptian Passover, and all others as *Pesach shel dorot*, the Passover of the generations. I will always think of Passover 1990 in Novosibirsk as a primal Pesach, much closer to Egypt than all my others.

The only outside ritual objects we had to supply to Morocco were slaughterers' knives, produced in Israel or America. On one of my entries to the country I was importing a variety of these blades in sizes ranging from small fowl knives to the largest ones, which are used for cattle. Making the package even heavier and more cumbersome were several sharpening stones from a special source in the US. I had informed my Casablanca office of this special baggage and requested that our driver arrive early to "smooth" my passage through Moroccan customs. As I wheeled my bags and the large package to customs, I noticed the conspicuous absence of the driver. I stalled and let several people ahead of me in the queue (not *de rigueur* in North Africa), but my predicament was drawing attention when I finally decided to go forward on my own. The customs officer was beginning to understand that my package was worth a very serious incentive when the driver suddenly appeared. Delayed by a highway accident, he immediately went into an aggressive mode, yelling at the officer about interfering with religious matters as grave as ritual slaughter. Did he not see that he was detaining a holy man?

Shame! Lots of apologies and many smiles, and I was whisked out with the knives and stones in tow.

We also provided tefillin to many distressed communities, but Morocco was not among those, since we had funded a small tefillin and mezuzah factory to provide employment for several men who had been trained to produce such ritual articles. I remember one large purchase in Jerusalem, when, on a whim, I decided to send one of the pairs of tefillin to be checked. That pair and, subsequently, the entire order (at many thousands of dollars) were declared unkosher for ritual use. That was when I discovered two disturbing facts about tefillin. The first was that simple tefillin at cheap prices for poor Jews were almost not available. All of the recent stress on strictness in religious law along with the affluence of certain communities had made simple (but still kosher) tefillin virtually non-existent. And the second sad fact was that this situation had produced a black market in fake tefillin that looked like the real thing and were obviously produced by so-called "religious Jews." I wished that our Casablanca factory, one of the last places producing simple tefillin, could have supplied the quantities we needed in other countries.

Tefillin always remind me of a trip to a small mining city in Siberia, Kemerova, home to a few hundred Jews. The locals showed me pictures of their attempt at a bar mitzvah of a local boy. They had heard about tefillin and seen pictures, but there were none in town. Accordingly, they produced a reasonable facsimile of black ribbons and cardboard and photographed the boy wearing them. It was all so innocent and touching. Like the matzot mentioned above, I kept thinking that their artificial tefillin were worth more in God's eyes than the most expensive pair one could buy in Jerusalem or in Brooklyn.

There were many moments when organized religion and its structure and rules came into conflict with the pure spirituality of simple folk. For Russian Jews who had as a model of religion the Russian Orthodox Church, entering a synagogue of the early 1990s was not an inspiring event. We must remember that during the Soviet period when clothes were dark and shabby, the air in most apartments was fetid and life was dreary, the music, scents, and vestments of the Church were a spiritual escape. The synagogues had little or no music, the few congregants were as shabbily dressed as everyone else, there were no rabbis in vestments, and the place was usually dirty and decrepit. It is actually a miracle that anyone with a soul turned up in the early synagogues of the FSU.

There were a few rabbis sent by Chasidic and other groups who managed to build significant synagogue life in communities that had had no exposure to religion for decades. I remember one young Chabad rabbi in Krasnajarsk who, without pastoral training, realized that compassion and love were his most important teachings. The Jews loved him because he loved them and put their emotional needs first.

While in Morocco synagogue life and the rhythm of the calendar were linked to religious law, there were some unique extra-legal moments which had a powerful effect on the local Jews and on me as a participant-observer. As is well known, Moroccan Jews, like their Moslem neighbors, venerate the graves of saints (*tzaddikim*, righteous persons). There is a long history in North Africa of identifying the graves of righteous people (the majority are men, but there are some notable women) and visiting them in order to commune with the spirit of the saint. As I mentioned elsewhere, some Jews even built small vacation huts near the graves so that they could visit for long periods. On the anniversary of the death of the tzaddik and on Lag ba-Omer (a festive day between Passover and Shavuot), large celebrations called *hilloulot* took place at the graves of the most popular tzaddikim.

On one occasion I spent the night at the Ouezzane cemetery, gravesite of Rabbi Amram Ben Diwan, and not being able to sleep because of the cold, I went for a walk. In the middle of the night I witnessed women sitting by the grave and talking to the saint. While none of this behavior is rooted in halachic practice, it is mainstream to the folk religion of Moroccan Jews and an important element in their communal spirituality.

Another illustration of the spiritual nature of Moroccan Jewry comes from one of their leaders, Rabbi Aharon Monsonego, head of the Ozar HaTorah school and the current Grand Rabbin of Morocco, a humble man revered by all. When I visited Morocco during the Gulf War in 1991, the tension in the streets was so high that my former contact at the police offered to walk with me on Shabbat as I went from the synagogue to friends' homes and back to the hotel. Although the King had sided with the Americans, many of the populace supported Iraq and Saddam Hussein. The Jews were especially uncomfortable, and Rabi Aharon (his only title) was sensitive to their needs. He spoke on Shabbat in the synagogue about friendship, citing numerous Biblical and Talmudic sources that all spoke of the value of human friendship. He encouraged his flock to invite each other for meals and conversation around the table. It was a talk devoid of religious law and obligations but filled with love and compassion; and it was received by Jews who valued his words like gold. I later asked Rabi Aharon for his sources and I cherish the notes he gave me. I have used them myself many times since.

As I wrote above, it was difficult for many Russian Jews to find themselves spiritually within the framework of Jewish religious practice. I am certain that we lost several souls to the Russian Orthodox Church and to western missionaries, who were very active throughout the FSU. Those who endeavored to find their Jewish path were often quite creative. I cited the artificial tefillin above, and I remember a description of a Jewish funeral that was equally moving. A woman who chaired a community organization in Khabarovsk described what she did to bury a fellow Jew. She gathered thirteen men (sic) and read relevant lines from a prayer book she had recently purchased in Moscow. She wanted to know what I thought of her rabbinic functions.

Realizing how important Jewish burial and mourning rites were to the Russian Jews we were encountering, the JDC staff prepared a manual of these customs for use in new communities that were reviving their religious lives. In one town, when I told an old man that we had this manual available, he asked whether we could also provide tachrichim, burial shrouds. In his eyes I saw that he was thinking of his own death and burial. The manual would be of little use to him, but shrouds would permit him to die as a Jew despite the former Soviet repression that prevented him from living as a Jew for so long.

It was in India that I also sensed a kind of profound spiritual connection that went beyond the legal obligations of religious life. I was at a community celebration in Bombay, where the main speaker was a former police chief, a Bene Israel Jew. He spoke lovingly of the memory of his mother reciting *kriat shema* (the central Jewish prayer) to him every night as he went to sleep. This was a highly assimilated Indian Jew who had risen to great heights in the civil service, but was powerfully connected to his people and his religion through his mother's spiritual instruction. He was proud to speak of it in public and he openly showed his sentiment. While the origins of the Bene Israel Jews are somewhat clouded by history, their spiritual connection to each other, to God, and to Jews around the world is plainly evident.

One of our Melton candidates being interviewed in Moscow told us that his re-connection to Jewish life was an internal aliyah (a Hebrew word meaning ascent, but used for immigration to Israel). He wasn't making excuses for not moving to Israel; he was describing an ascent of his soul to a new level of consciousness. Another candidate for the Melton Jewish educators' program in Jerusalem summed it up even more profoundly. He said, "There is religion and there is belief. I am a believer."

CHAPTER NINE

KASHRUT

WHILE OTHER ASPECTS of Jewish religion and spirituality have just been explored in the previous chapter, kashrut, the dietary laws, figured in many of the experiences in a variety of field locations.

In Morocco, kashrut was part of the natural flow of Jewish life and was practiced by almost every Jew in the community. There is no doubt that the rabbis and teachers kept a stricter version of the dietary laws than the average household, but one had to search far and wide for a Jewish home that mixed meat and dairy or that bought its meat from anyone other than a kosher butcher. In the small Casablanca community of ten thousand Jews, there were, in 1981, eighteen kosher butchers. The major hotels had kosher kitchens for catering Jewish events, and there were a few kosher restaurants.

Of course, there was no kashrut in the USSR. Those of us who concerned ourselves with such matters traveled with as much food as clothing. In 1989 and 1990 one could manage a meal of canned gefilte fish in a back room of the Choral Synagogue in Moscow, but no other facilities existed.

I remember a Siberian Hebrew teacher who had just found out about the Jewish dietary laws and wanted to observe what she could in order to be a part of the Jewish people. From her description of the effort, I don't think God or Torah had anything to do with her decision; it was an ethnic move. She banned meat from the house except for her husband ("who needed it"), but she salted his unkosher flesh before she cooked it! She had heard that there were some issues with cheese, and she asked me if she should continue eating it. I had visions of her wasting away the more she learned about kashrut.

When the first summer camps were organized in the FSU, there wasn't even a thought about kosher food. Soviet parents thought of camp as a place in the country with fresh air, sports, and lots of healthy food (read: protein). The first time an attempt was made at eliminating meat (since kosher meat was unavailable), parents actually drove to the camp to protest. This was merely a cultural conflict. The parents knew nothing about kashrut, and the foreign camp organizers knew just as much about Soviet camping traditions. Of course, when secular Israelis organized a camp, there was no problem using the local meat.

I remember an Israel Independence Day party organized by some wonderful Israeli volunteers at which each little morsel of pork and cheese had a tiny Israeli flag stuck in it.

In contrast, one of the great scandals of the summer camps in Immouzer, Morocco, was the time that the cook found a non-kosher fish (one without scales and fins) among the food order that had just arrived from the market in Fes. One would have thought that the end of the world was upon us from the screams heard from the kitchen.

In 1985 the JDC funded a program to train six local men as rabbis for the Moroccan community. As they approached the end of their studies, it was decided that they should spend several months in a Jerusalem yeshiva in order to get their *semicha* (ordination) from the Sephardic Chief Rabbi of Israel. I was asked to meet them at the airport and to escort them to their yeshiva in Jerusalem, which I did. The next morning, when I arrived at the yeshiva to check on their arrangements, I walked into a tempest. Dairy is not an item in Moroccan Jewish cuisine, and the evening meal the night before had been pizza. Since these six Moroccan men were used to elaborate dinners of many courses, the pizza itself was a culinary shock, but added to that was their discovery that dairy was served from the same kitchen as meat. My rabbis-to-be decided immediately on a hunger strike.

Imagine telling the head of a yeshiva that his kashrut was being questioned by some students from Morocco. It took a tour of the kitchen, demonstrating the three sections; meat, dairy, and pareve (neutral) plus a long explanation of what constituted a decent meal outside of Morocco before the men consented to eat, but I am certain that they never really made peace with either the menu or the level of kashrut. Most Moroccan homes I visited had but one set of dishes, with no category of dairy or pareve in their kitchen repertoire.

The single most embarrassing story about kashrut in the field took place in Paris. Our Paris office was not known for its kosher kitchen, but one summer day a meeting had been scheduled that involved myself and another colleague who ate kosher food. As a surprise for us, the office went to great pains to order in a sumptuous lunch from a kosher caterer; chicken, salads, cold meats, and wine. The only problem was that it was the seventeenth of Tammuz on the Hebrew calendar, a fast day. My colleague and I were hard put to explain, especially since no one else in the office had ever heard of this particular fast. We promised to break the fast that evening in our hotel rooms on the food that we hastily packed in foil.

The kosher slaughter of cattle in most countries permits the use of only the front section of the animal. This is based on Genesis 32:33, an ancient prohibition involving meat in the vicinity of the sciatic nerve. In some communities, there is a butchering procedure called *nikkur*, which permits the use of the hindquarters. Morocco is one of those communities, and the Jews of Morocco have always enjoyed the better cuts of meat from the back of the cow and lamb. At one point, it became clear to the rabbis in Morocco that the butchers had forgotten the proper technique for *nikkur*, and a training program was set up with demonstrations on freshly slaughtered animals. None of my colleagues in the field funded anything like this in their respective countries.

Nikkur was also practiced in Melilla, a Spanish enclave on the northern coast of Morocco with a Jewish community of some one thousand souls. After their venerable old rabbi died, we arranged for a new rabbi to serve the community. In his short stay he managed to declare the local butcher ignorant of the proper procedure for *nikkur*, and only front-end meat became permitted. While many of the local Jews did not respect this rabbi, his ruling became law and their diet changed overnight. Their butcher did not know how to properly cut the available meat, since hindquarters were always preferred and the other meat was usually ground up for *kefta* and stuffing. I found myself writing for a consulting butcher to help them out; a quaint letter that is still in my files.

The funniest incident concerning kashrut occurred in the ninth arrondissement of Paris, a neighborhood with many kosher Tunisian restaurants. One of them was my favorite for a quick, inexpensive meal on visits to Paris and when I later moved there. One evening, the place was empty except for the Muslim waiter, two American tourists who had not realized what kind of restaurant they had entered, and myself. A bit of cultural translation was required. The owner and the *mashgiach* (kashrut supervisor) were absent. Then, in walked a strange couple – a Moroccan Jewish man and a woman who was obviously not of the same faith. They sat down side by side and commenced to get quite intimate for such a public place. My friend, the waiter, took their order, and they continued their little intimacies. The waiter approached my table and explained that they had ordered wine, but without a Jewish employee present, the wine could not be opened. (This, a bit of complex Jewish law regarding the consumption of wine.) Would I be so kind? "*M'kein mushkil,*" I answered ("No problem" in Moroccan Arabic). After opening the bottle, I was prevailed upon one more time. Repeating all the usual French apologies several times, the waiter asked me, "Would Monsieur please pour the wine" (another prohibition)? Now I found myself, towel in hand, pouring wine for this quite literally loving couple, the male half of which could not see himself eating in a non-kosher restaurant while dating this obviously non-Jewish woman!

As mysterious as the dietary laws are, they had unified the Jewish people until the modern period, during which most Jews, both in the Diaspora and in Israel, abandoned them. The Moroccan Jews, an ancient community with little divergence from the traditions of the past, kept these laws naturally, with little reflection. As for the Soviet Union, at the time of the Russian Revolution, most Jews in the area were still connected to Jewish tradition while others chose the paths of enlightenment, assimilation, or Communism. Seven decades of Soviet repression severed almost all USSR Jews from kashrut and every other symbol of their faith. Yet despite the Soviet pressure, some central Asian communities managed to keep a diet that was more or less in line with the ancient ways. There were stories of Asian mountain villages where kosher slaughter existed until the last *shochet* died. In 1991 Kishinev still had an old *shochet*, who, inspired by the end of Communism, was training a young man to replace him. I saw an old woman complain that she wanted her chicken slaughtered only by the old man, whom she trusted. When I asked the young man whether he needed anything, he asked for two things: a slaughtering manual and a bride. The joke requires explanation. The slaughtering manual is entitled *Simla Chadasha* ("new dress" in Hebrew), and the bride is required so that the slaughterer will be a stable member of the community.

To this day, the dispersed Moroccans keep their faith with kashrut. Will the FSU Jews find a place in their various forms of Jewish life for kashrut and the other customs of our spiritual heritage? That question remains to be answered.

CHAPTER TEN

MISSIONS

ONE OF THE DUTIES of any JDC country director is to lead study missions of visiting UJA or JDC lay leaders. These two-to four-day visits can be very useful to the JDC, UJA, and local federations in demonstrating how charitable donations are used in the field. Surprisingly, they are also useful to JDC staff in that the planning of such missions compelled us to see our programs from the perspectives of outsiders.

Of course, not every country director relished the idea of taking three full days out of a busy schedule to act as tour guide to visiting innocents. The local leadership also tired of constantly being available for visiting leaders. The director of a French Jewish organization once asked me about the many requests he got from New York UJA to escort important leaders on tours of Jewish Paris. He wanted to know where the followers were!

My first mission was thrust on me by complete surprise that quickly escalated to shock. When I arrived in Casablanca in August of 1981, one of the first bits of information I swallowed was that the current country director was leaving for vacation in November and that I was to lead a group of UJA women around the country. I had no idea what that entailed, but I was aware that I knew nothing about either Morocco or its JDC program of operations.

What I encountered was a dedicated group of women who devoted themselves to UJA work, who sincerely wanted to see our projects and just as sincerely wanted to shop until they dropped; which one of them did down the stairs of our office building. That was the trip that honed my souk bargaining skills, which were critically important to both my mission duties and to my growing collection of Berber carpets.

When, in preparation for this first mission, I visited one of the kindergartens that was meant to be one of the sites on the tour of Casablanca, I was somewhat shocked to see a picture of Jesus on the wall. When I asked the rabbi/principal what the picture was doing in a Jewish kindergarten, he explained innocently that it was a picture of a shepherd and his flock. That it was, but I knew the figure to be that of Jesus. (The halo helped!) My wise colleague asked how I knew what Jesus looked like, and that was an early indication of a community untouched by Christian symbolism. I merely requested that the poster be removed for several days.

Evening entertainment was always a problem on Moroccan missions, since our programs were daytime visits and the evenings were free. Most tourists to Marrakech spend at least one night eating dinner in a Berber tent watching a replication for tourists of the old Berber victory celebrations, a Fantasia. Since UJA mission meals had to be kosher, this could not be an organized event on a mission itinerary. I found a Jew in the Fantasia business, offered him new utensils and dishes, and with the help of the local rabbi, created a new UJA program – a kosher Fantasia. This included roast lamb, couscous, snake charmers, native dancers, and Berber horsemen firing muskets!

When I organized this event for a mission from Baltimore in 1983 (just after my wedding), I got a frantic call several weeks before the mission (and hours before my wedding) from the Baltimore Federation demanding that I cancel the snake charmers. It seems that a member of the delegation had a severe phobia of snakes, pictures of snakes, and any reference to snakes. All of my pleading about the harmlessness of these particular serpents and their distance from the audience were to no avail. Call off the snakes, they said, or we call off the mission. From Toronto I immediately called JDC headquarters in New York and dictated a telex to be sent to the Casablanca office.

> FOR BALTIMORE MISSION FANTASIA, CANCEL SNAKES. REPEAT NO SNAKES. WILL EXPLAIN LATER. EPI.

The telex operator wanted to know if this was a new secret money transfer code she didn't recognize.

On another occasion, a New York JDC executive was enthusiastically "selling" a Moroccan mission to a new board member and mentioned that I had arranged a kosher Fantasia in Marrakech. (Sounds pretty enticing, *n'est-ce pas?*) Shocked, the fellow asked if the mission ate kosher food and was answered affirmatively. "Oh, my wife and I don't eat kosher food. We can't go." And they didn't.

One of the great difficulties we had with UJA leadership was our concern for security in Morocco. Since His Majesty King Hassan II was overtly philo-Semitic and just as overtly anti-Zionist, we made it a practice to distance our office and our programs from any reference to Israel. In fact, in telex traffic we called Israel Texas. (Once, a new JDC executive director wondered why I suggested a Hebrew in-service course for Moroccan teachers in Dallas!) Consequently, we asked UJA visitors to refrain from talking about Israel or Zionism while in Morocco.

Nothing could have been more ridiculous. These were people whose entire lives centered around their work for Israel. It was what bound them to each other. In most cases, Morocco was a pre-mission followed by time in Israel. We would be traveling on a bus from Casablanca to Rabat with a tour guide, when suddenly someone would mention Israel. "This road looks just like the outskirts of Beersheva." Then someone would remember my request and shush up the talk. "Epi asked us to say 'Texas.'" Then everyone would laugh. And, of course, the tour guide had much to report that evening.

In case any readers should suspect me of paranoia, the tea incident in Marrakech will illustrate the justification for my concerns. The president of the Marrakech community begged me to permit a mission to be invited to the Pasha's office for a formal tea. The Pasha of Marrakech is always a political personality very close to the king, and the JDC shied away from such exposure. Seeing that this was important to the local community, I approved the tea with the condition that there be no reporters or photos. We were met by klieg lights, local television, and a photo crew, but I could hardly cancel the visit on the steps of the Pasha's office. The meeting was graciously hospitable, and I soon forgot my fears. A few weeks later I was called by the security officer at the U.S. Consulate in Casablanca and informed that the Consul General needed to see me immediately. He and his staff showed me an article in the local Arab press about my visit with the Pasha. It noted that the organization I represented, the Joint, was well known for its ties with the CIA and the Mossad. After that, I never had any doubts regarding the ubiquity of the secret police in Morocco.

Language and cultural divides were also the source of some funny mission moments. While escorting a group from some American city on a tour of our home for the aged in Casablanca, an older woman stopped by the bed of a very old resident and started a conversation in Yiddish. This particular resident was from a mountain community and spoke a Berber dialect. Even our staff had difficulty communicating with her in her limited knowledge of Arabic. When I explained that Yiddish was not one of her current languages, the visitor responded with some anger, "That's what's wrong with you young Jews; you know nothing. All old

Jews speak Yiddish." I tried to explain, but she just kept talking in Yiddish, louder and louder as tourists are wont to do. Finally, to get some relief, the ancient resident nodded and sighed. "See, I told you so!"

One mission arrived for Simchat Torah and expected either a neo-Chasidic celebration that they were used to in their Conservative synagogue back home or something resembling the crowds outside Moscow's Choral Synagogue in the late Soviet period. While Moroccans in Israel do celebrate Simchat Torah with some Ashkenazic influence, the traditional Torah celebrations in Morocco are on Shavuot, the festival of Mount Sinai, not on Simchat Torah, a late addition to our holiday calendar. Moroccan hospitality being what it is, the local rabbi accommodated the tourists by adding a few songs and dances to the service.

By the way, the Shavuot tradition is subtly beautiful. Before removing the Torah from its ark, a long marriage contract (*ketubbah*) is read that weds the Jewish people to God with the Torah as the sign of the everlasting love between them.

One of the very best missions I ever led was a tiny group from the JDC board who were brave enough to visit our new Siberian communities. If I have had my fun above in recounting some of the piquant vignettes of missions, let me use the example of this mission to make it clear that the missions to JDC field operations were of utmost importance and that most of the time and energy went into a profound exchange of information and sentiment. North American Jewish leaders, professional and lay alike, learned a great deal from these trips and were re-inspired in their work to raise the funds necessary for our activities to continue. The locals, for their part, were moved by the presence of caring Jews and inspired by the dedication of these "distant relatives" who could easily do other things with their time.

This 1997 mission to Siberia consisted of many visits to the infancy of Jewish communal life; welfare programs with visits to rotting Soviet apartments, new youth groups singing the latest Israeli music, abandoned cemeteries, Jews reciting *Kabbalat Shabbat* for the very first time, and Sunday schools unlike anything in New Jersey.

At the very end of a long day in Irkutsk on the last day of the mission, we all decided to sit down in the hotel lounge for a summary meeting. I ordered Cokes all around. Just as our Siberian area representative, himself a Lithuanian Israeli, was about to pay the waiter, one of the mission women said that they all preferred Diet Cokes. Surprisingly, they had diet drinks imported from Japan and, now impressed by the needs of this group, the waiter provided tall glasses with ice and filled each with the new beverages. Ready to pay for the second time, our representative was cut off by the remark that our group didn't use the local ice and preferred to drink from the bottle. What to do? Pay the fellow and order bottled diet drinks, no glasses, no ice. When the third order arrived, it was noted that the drinks were warm. No refrigerator here; hence the ice. Nobody drank a drop. When my Lithuanian colleague paid for this round, he looked at me in utter dismay and said: "I just paid for eighteen drinks and no one has had a single sip!"

My wife always loved this story because both perspectives make sense in their respective contexts. The travelers have refrigerators at home filled with every possible kind of drink and their local supermarket has one hundred times that variety. Choice is their right, their custom, and their default setting. The locals lived forever on their adaptability to no choice. How long would an American GI have lasted under the daily conditions of a Soviet soldier in World War II? No one ever asked me what I wanted to drink in a Russian house. Drinks were served and everyone drank whatever appeared that day in the store; when there were drinks at all.

The president of the Marrakech Jewish community was an especially gracious host and his abundant hospitality got me into deep trouble on one mission, a wonderful group from my hometown of Toronto. The plan was to eat a Friday evening Shabbat dinner at his villa in the new town of Marrakech, Gueliz. Three of the couples on the mission were observant Orthodox Jews who needed to be convinced that his home was kosher. Since I knew the family very well, knew the wife to be very careful about kashrut, and knew the son to be connected to Lubavitch Chasidism I could easily vouch for the kitchen. What I forgot was that this particular Moroccan Jew had a loose understanding of Shabbat observance and decided to meet the group on his porch with a video camera and lights (We already know of his love for cameras and lights from the story above!) at an hour which was already well into Shabbat. This open desecration of the Sabbath did not impress my Orthodox mission participants (or myself), and brought the kashrut of the meal into question. Faced with the possibility that several key guests were about to leave and go hungry, I introduced the strictly observant wife of the host, along with her visibly Orthodox son, and all went well.

Trivial as these incidents are, they point to a micro-observation of the Jewish family working out its ethnic, spiritual, and cultural differences, sensing the tension created by such differences and, at the same time, aspiring to *shelom bayit*, a peaceful household.

CHAPTER ELEVEN

A LESSON FROM THE SIXTEENTH CENTURY

ONE FRIDAY NIGHT in Casablanca, my host, Rabbi Aharon Monsonego, asked me if I knew that the Friday evening hymn, Lecha Dodi, was about love. As mentioned earlier, Rabi Aharon (his title for the entire community even after he became the Moroccan Chief Rabbi) was the director of the Ozar HaTorah Schools in Morocco. Born in Fes and educated in France, his father, Rabi Yedidya Monsonego, was the Chief Rabbi at the time. Bien sûr, love is the obvious theme of this sixteenth-century hymn, the centerpiece of the Friday evening synagogue service. But Rabi Aharon was not talking about human love or even about divine love. He wanted to point out that this great poem, revered by every Jewish community in the world, was about l'amour municipale (!) – love between two cities.

At the time, Tzefat (Safed), where the poem was written by Shlomo ha-Levi Alkabetz, was prospering as a Jewish city. It was full of students, teachers, halachists, kabbalists, philosophers, and poets, most of whom were composing new texts and novel customs. Jerusalem, the holiest city of the land of Israel and much more ancient a city than Tzefat, was not enjoying the same vitality in the sixteenth century. It was mostly in ruins. According to Rabi Aharon, the hymn is the voice of Tzefat declaring her love and devotion to Jerusalem.

> Sanctuary of the King, royal city, arise.
> Come forth from your ruins.
> Too long have you dwelt in the valley of tears.
> He will show you abundant mercy....

> The Lord's glory is revealed in you....
> Why are you downcast? Why do you moan?
> The afflicted of my people will be sheltered by you.
> The city shall be rebuilt in its own place....

> Come, my friend, to meet the bride;
> Let us welcome the Shabbat together.

It was that night in Casablanca that I came to realize that this original reading of *Lecha Dodi* was the story of the American Jewish Joint Distribution Committee and its mission. The powerful Jewish Diaspora community of North America has been helping other communities around the world, most of them older, wiser, and once richer than American Jewry, but now in need of assistance.

Throughout my years in North Africa, Western Europe, Israel, and the Former Soviet Union I came back to that Friday evening text again and again. I could not engage in helping another community without recognizing both the powerful Jewry that sent me and the hidden strengths of the Jews who now needed our help.

Whether in the midst of a disintegrating ancient community or within the enthusiasm and complexity of reconnecting "new" Jews to their lost Judaism, their own people, and their own land, the overwhelming power of community was evident in every act that my colleagues and I performed.

While community life was the leitmotif of our work, it was played out in the time-honored realms of Jewish values that I listed at the outset as our operational work ethos: Talmud Torah, tzedakah, chesed, ahavat Yisrael, tikkun olam, and the pluralism of elu ve-elu.

> Shake off your dust, arise!
> Put on your glorious garments, my people….
> Be not ashamed or confounded….
> Your God will rejoice over you as a groom over his bride….
>
> Come, my friend, to meet the bride;
> Let us welcome the Shabbat together.

Seymour Epstein on the Amur River in eastern Siberia, 1990s.

GLOSSARY

Aide Scolaire – One of the social-service organizations in Morocco

AIU – Alliance Israélite Universelle, one of the Jewish school systems in Morocco

Appel – The United Jewish Appeal in France

Buncher – A leadership training program run by JDC

C.I. – Communauté Israelite, the central community organization in Morocco

DEJJ – Départment Educatif de la Jeunesse Juive, a French and Moroccan Jewish youth group

EIM – Eclaireurs Israelites du Maroc (Scouts)

FSJU – Fonds Social Juif Unifié, the central social welfare organization of French Jewry

FSU – Former Soviet Union

Ittihad – The Arabic name of the AIU in Morocco

Mellah – The Jewish quarter in a Moroccan city, town, or village

Naaleh-16 – A program of the Jewish Agency for Israel designed to bring teens to study in Israel before their parents immigrate

Ozar HaTorah – One of the Jewish school systems in Morocco

Rabbi, Rabi – A Moroccan rabbi is called Rabi by the locals.

REK – An early Jewish communal organization in the FSU

SUT – Soviet Union Team, the JDC term for the FSU operating team; the acronym also refers to the meetings of the team

Vaad – The first Perestroika-period Russian Jewish umbrella organization

ABOUT THE AUTHOR

Dr. Seymour Epstein (Epi) (b. January 3, 1946, Toronto, Canada), has been active in every aspect of Jewish education, formal and informal, for more than thirty-five years. He worked at United Synagogue Day School in Toronto, helping to found an experimental high school there in 1971. From 1973 to 1978 he was an assistant professor at McGill University, where he directed the Jewish Teacher Training Program of Montreal. He also directed Camp Ramah in Canada for three summers.

In 1981, Dr. Epstein moved to Morocco in order to become the educational consultant for the American Jewish Joint Distribution Committee in Casablanca. Since then, he has been involved in JDC work in Morocco, Western Europe, and the former Soviet Union. He served as the JDC's Director of Jewish Education and was responsible for community development in Siberia, Russia.

Having returned to Toronto, Dr. Epstein serves as the senior vice president of the UJA Federation Centre for Enhancement of Jewish Education.

He and his wife, Cheryl, have two children, Yoni and Sarit.